A CHRISTIAN PAINTER OF THE

NINETEENTH CENTURY

RIVINGTONS

London ........................................ *Waterloo Place*
Oxford ........................................ *High Street*
Cambridge ........................................ *Trinity Street*

[B—33]

# A CHRISTIAN PAINTER

OF

# The Nineteenth Century

BEING THE

*LIFE OF HIPPOLYTE FLANDRIN*

BY THE AUTHOR OF

"A DOMINICAN ARTIST," "LIFE OF S. FRANCIS DE SALES,"

ETC. ETC.

New York

POTT, YOUNG, AND COMPANY

COOPER UNION, FOURTH AVENUE

MDCCCLXXV

# Prefatory Note

I CANNOT commit this little book to the public without expressing gratitude to the kindness and courtesy of M. le Vicomte Henri Delaborde, who has so freely given me the benefit of all his resources in connection with Flandrin's works and life. If these pages should lead to his friend and countryman being better known among ourselves, and to his noble example being followed, it will, I know, more than reward him.

# Contents

# A CHRISTIAN PAINTER OF THE NINETEENTH CENTURY.

ALL those who are interested in Modern Art, especially those who look upon mural decoration as one of its noblest objects, and who desire to see the walls of our churches an abiding lesson to the eye of the faithful, are acquainted with the name of Hippolyte Flandrin, and more or less with his works. But among the numbers who have admired and studied his paintings in Saint Germain des Prés, Saint Severin, or Saint Vincent de Paul, at Paris, the Church of Saint Paul at Nîmes, or that of Ainay at Lyons, few probably know anything concerning the painter, or the mind which prompted that skilful hand to trace the devout imaginations which have won for Flandrin the name of the Fra Angelico of our day.

It was not a life of great events, or strange picturesque combinations like some of the early masters, whose lives seem when read as artistic as their works; neither was he a *dévot*, to be held up as an unusual and specially edifying instance of artist-piety. Nevertheless, there was that about Hippolyte Flandrin's life which makes it worthy of record, and interesting to those who take pleasure in tracing a true, honest, manly, straightforward character through the toils and difficulties which inevitably beset every life lived with a clear, noble, deliberate intention of working out a vocation in God's Service, be that vocation what it may. And the purity and truthfulness and manliness with which Flandrin followed his artist's vocation, —bearing up stedfastly under the pressure of poverty and disappointment, and, while without any special profession of piety, cleaving with a true resolute heart to the plain duties of a Christian life, come what might,—are a deep lesson and encouragement to all, most particularly, one would imagine, to the numerous brotherhood of artists following in his steps; and as assuredly many of them share in his poverty and his trials, may not his example help some of them to share in that which was his strength as a man and his inspiration as an artist, namely, his pure life and his God-fearing ways?

Hippolyte Flandrin inherited a love of art. In early days his father too had aimed at becoming a painter; and, after a few years spent in a house of business, he threw up his occupation, ambitiously hoping to become an historical painter in what was known at that time as the School of Lyons, his native place. But either the father's talent was inferior in its kind, or it could not contend against the disadvantages of a tardy education, and Flandrin the elder soon found that, if he wished to find bread for the seven little mouths which were gathered around him to be filled, he must take to the less dignified line of miniature painting, and indeed reckon himself fortunate when by that he could eke out the scanty means which alone he possessed besides—consisting of the rent of a small house in the Rue des Bouchers at Lyons, which he shared with his sister. The fourth of the hungry birds in the Flandrin nest was Hippolyte, born March 23, 1809. Both his brothers were art aspirants too, and the younger one, Paul Flandrin, still living, is reckoned as one of the first landscape painters in France.

Their mother had experienced a good deal of the uncertainty and depressing hopelessness of a disappointed artist's career; and though she resigned herself somewhat reluctantly to its adoption by her eldest son Auguste, five years older than Hippolyte, when it became a question of the younger boys following the same unprofitable calling, the good house-mother fairly set her back to the wall, refusing to listen to any sentiment or artistic pleading, and declared that one painter was quite enough in the family,—it was enough to have one son the victim of uncertainty, caprice and disappointment: she would have no more forsooth! No, indeed! Hippolyte should not be tempted into the studio—he should be apprenticed to an honest silk merchant; and as to little Paul, he should set to work at the tailor's trade; and the shop where he was to learn his business was forthwith fixed upon. Meanwhile, probably owing to the scanty purse at home, the boys were not sent to school, and having, in common with so many of their age, a hot military fever upon them, Hippolyte and Paul spent most of their time in close attendance upon the regiments quartered in Lyons. Not a march or parade did they miss;—the barrack and the *champ de manœuvre* were both studied with absorbing interest; and when they came home from their day's pursuit, the evenings were spent in drawing all they had seen, one helping another in rendering detail accurately; and happy the day was to them when, by some fortunate chance, any military illustrations—lithographic or engraved—fell into their hands as a supreme authority. Hippolyte's military ardour never departed.[1] Later on he was fully prepared, in case of war breaking out, to enter the Garde Mobile; and one of the first works which brought him any remuneration—after all it was only thirty-five francs!—was the portrait of a gendarme, painted soon after his arrival in Paris.

[1] In the Journal of his last days in Rome, Flandrin's admiration for and interest in his country's soldiers comes out strongly.

At this time the boys had no higher aim than to imitate Horace Vernet, or Charlet, and their battle-pieces, their field-days, parades and military scenes acquired a certain reputation for the "petits Flandrin," somewhat to their mother's dismay, who dreaded nothing so much as to see them led astray by the pernicious snare, as she believed it to be, of an artist's life. But in vain poor Madame Flandrin pleaded the cause of tailoring and silk mercery,—her sons found a powerful advocate on their side, who succeeded in silencing, if not in convincing, their mother. In 1821, when the boys were eleven and twelve years old, the sculptor Foyatier came to Lyons, and renewed his acquaintance with the Flandrin family. He was a living witness against the maternal advocacy; for eighteen years ago, Foyatier—now a successful artist, established in Paris, and on his way at the actual moment to Rome,—this same sculptor had come eighteen years before from the country village where his previous life had been spent herding sheep, and had induced a vendor of statuettes (supplied chiefly to religious houses) to take him as an apprentice, and from this humble beginning he had advanced to his present position. Foyatier found no difficulty in convincing the father and sons that the latter would do well to despise the prospects of trade and follow the leadings of art; and even the prudent mother was not invulnerable to the argument of personal success, and the prestige of an *homme arrivé*, which gave force to Foyatier's words. He pleaded and argued so successfully, that, before he went on to Italy, he saw the two little fellows installed as pupils in a studio directed by a painter named Magnin, and a better-known artist, the sculptor Legendre-Héral. And so the boys were launched upon the sea of art, and for a while the skies were clear and the sunshine cheered them. Hippolyte studied both from the antique and from the living model, and, still aiming to become a painter of battle-fields, he was encouraged in that line by his masters, who looked approvingly upon the sketches of military subjects which he often made from nature when out of the studio. But before long Magnin went to Italy, where he died, and Flandrin, whose ambition was whetted by what he had already learned, sought and found admittance into the École de Saint Pierre, the Academy of Fine Arts of Lyons. Here he studied for seven years under Révoil, then director of the atelier, and a diligent, unwearied, painstaking study it was; supplementing the appointed hours of work with as much private toil as he could manage, especially the study of animals—going daily to one of the faubourgs where he had an opportunity of drawing the latter from the life, all with a view to his supposed vocation in the military line. But meanwhile the pressure of poverty made itself heavily felt at home, and in every possible way the two boys, who were the most dutiful and affectionate of sons, strove to lighten their parents' burden, to which they were conscious of adding by the pursuit of their dearly-loved profession, instead of following a lucrative trade. It is touching to find them striving in every possible way to earn a few sous; one time drawing little vignettes for the shops where cheap pictures are sold, another time executing lithography, and gladly selling a stone with twenty finished subjects for fifteen francs, even designing rebuses and bonbon cases for the confectioner;—anything whatsoever that could bring in but a handful of grist to the slowly dropping family mill.

Moreover, there was another object for which sous and centimes were to be scraped together. Of course Paris was their great aim and aspiration; the paradise of imagination, where Vernets and Davids, Murillos and Raffaeles, and all the treasures of art, which as yet were to them only myths or faintly shadowed forth by more or less imperfect engravings and lithographs, might be seen and worshipped; the world of reality, where the first living masters might be found to teach willing pupils to excel themselves. Yes, to Paris Hippolyte and Paul Flandrin intended fully to go; but how were the funds ever to be obtained for carrying out their intentions? Never mind! their hearts were in it; and when a resolute earnest lad sets himself steadily to work out his heartfelt vocation, somehow or other he is sure to do it. So, little by little, a sum was hoarded up, small indeed, but sufficient, as the young Flandrins hoped and believed, for their actual necessities, and therewith they made the important plunge into the world. It was a humble start, for the journey alone would pretty well have swallowed up their little store if they had not chosen the slow but cheap way of travelling, and walked to Paris. Flandrin's own boyish account of the great event is the best portrait of what he was then as a lad of twenty.

"PARIS, *April* 11, 1829.

"Mon cher Papa et ma chère Maman,—There is an end to all your anxiety; we have arrived here safe and sound, and I will tell you all about our journey. I am sure you have thought a great deal about us all the time, but not more than we have thought of you. When we left Auguste at Dijon, sorrowfully enough, we took the high road to Montbard. So far we had walked over a vast plain, about which Auguste is sure to have told you. By degrees the road became more desolate, and the air colder. We went uphill for three hours; the cheerful villages all disappeared, and we went between two woods of small oak trees, till at last we came down into a valley very like Bugey—high rocks, well wooded mountain sides, and a little river in the bottom. When we reached the opposite side we came into a very cold wind, which soon brought snow. It was nearly dark; we tried two lonely inns, but they could not, or would not, receive us, and we had to go on another mile to an inn, where we did very well for that night. The next day was splendid, but a hard frost; we slept at Montbard, a little town built on a sort of mamelon. I saw nothing remarkable there but a fine crenelated tower. Here the weather changed, and rain made the roads horrid, but at last we struggled through them, and got to Tonnerre to sleep. That was our fifth day from Lyons. The sixth day we went on twelve miles to La Roche, a village near Joigny, in perpetual storms of wind and rain, against which we had no means of defence except this." (Here comes a sketch by Paul of the two brothers cowering, half-sheltered, under a tree, with a legend beneath, "Ah si la maman nous voyait là!" and another, in which they are both squatting under a streaming umbrella, with the inscription, "à defaut d'arbres"). "So we waited patiently for a pause in the storm, talking of home the while. The seventh day a continuance of this weather induced us to go as far as Sens in a carriage, but I repented this heartily, for I was tremendously sick. Sens is to my mind a very pretty, clean, cheerful town, and the cathedral is magnificent. On the eighth day we slept at Moret, just on the borders of the forest of Fontainebleau, and the day after we went through the forest, beginning to find that we were nearing Paris by the good roads, the numerous villages, and quantity of carriages. At Fontainebleau we admired the grand château; the eagles are still all crowned with laurels, and here and there some fleurs de lys appear. Thence we went to Rys, only six miles from Paris, and the next day we got up, eagerly hoping soon to see it. But we went at least five miles without seeing anything. However, at last, from a rising ground, we saw the great city, and were very much struck with the *ensemble* which appeared; the domes of the Invalides and Panthéon, the towers of Notre Dame, and many others. But when we reached the city nothing astonished us; on the contrary, several things shocked me. I thought we should have been obliged to make our entry with flying colours, *i.e.* open umbrella; but instead of that the sun broke out, and the weather was beautiful. I must tell you all my impressions another time; but I have already seen the Vendôme Column. Oh, how fine it is! Our love to Uncle and Aunt Martin. As for you, we love you as much as we did at Lyons, and Auguste and Caroline too; we forget no one. Embrace every one of the family you see for us."

The first thing was to find a dwelling-place within

the compass of the brothers' very small means. After some toil in the shape of lodging-hunting, they found an unfurnished room in the Quai de la Cité, No. 13, on the fourth floor, which seemed to the young men very dear, its rent, though the room was small, being 140 francs for the year. In a letter to his father, Hippolyte gives an inventory of their furniture, which is soon transcribed. It consisted of a bedstead with paillasse and mattress, a table, two chairs, a candlestick, and a water-pot. "I nearly forgot the broom!" he adds, with the further assurance that he and Paul kept their little abode "as clean and tidy as possible." Their manner of life was as frugal and unsophisticated as the anxious parental hearts which brooded over them afar could have desired. "We get up at five o'clock and go out for a whiff of fresh air in the Luxembourg, which is not far, and then at six we set to work. At eight or nine we breakfast. Unfortunately, bread was never so dear as it is just now. Then we work till six in the evening. Our breakfasts cost five sous each, and we dine for fifteen sous apiece, which makes forty sous a day between us. We feed at a very clean restaurant, where we eat the simplest and plainest things we can get."

However, the brothers could not always achieve even such a dinner as this, and it not unfrequently happened that they were obliged to content themselves with three sous' worth of fried potatoes, bought on the Pont Neuf, and divided between the two! But there was no grumbling, no craving after self-indulgence. The two strong affections, love of art and love of their parents, made that impossible.

"You bade us not run into debt," Hippolyte writes: "oh! as to that you may be quite easy! I would rather make the greatest sacrifices. Be certain of your children's love. Far away as they are, they will do nothing which you could disapprove, and they will try to be a comfort to you." And again, on February 5, 1830, he says, "You bid us be economical. I assure you we are, for we do not spend more than fifteen or sixteen sous each on our daily food, and to do that one must needs be very careful. I don't think that since we came here we have spent one sou unprofitably. Indeed, we feel too strongly how much sacrifice you make for your sons, dear mother, in the money you send us, and you may be certain that we shall husband it to the very uttermost."

It was hard work to make both ends meet nevertheless, and at the end of three months Hippolyte says, "In spite of economy, our money melts fast; we work with all our might to earn something." And when Flandrin the father contrived with difficulty to send a hundred francs, hardly saved, to his boys, Hippolyte wrote warm thanks, adding, "I am afraid you must have pinched yourself to send it, and the thought grieves me. Oh! if only my longings were fulfilled, how I should delight in being able to help you! But I don't get on as I should like."

His home affections were very strong, and a letter from father or mother was one of the greatest delights that could gladden the young students. "You can't imagine the pleasure with which we get your letters," he writes (May 16, 1829). "It is an event which cheers us up, and is altogether an epoch to us." And writing to his brother Auguste, Hippolyte says: "I can't describe to you the intense longing I have to see and hug you, as well as *le papa et la maman.* Almost every night I am off to Lyons, and yesterday I was downright cross with Paul for waking me, because just then I was embracing you all. I was crying for joy. . . . Remember that we agreed to pray for one another every night. I never fail to do so, and I am quite sure our poor mother never fails either. She loves us so dearly, and she is such a long way off! Poor father and mother, your children are all scattered now!"

But the passionate home love tended to strengthen rather than diminish the other affection, which cannot be called its rival,—love of art. The original programme of the two brothers had not been carried out. They left Lyons with an introduction from Révoil, the director of that school of art, to Hersent, as also a recommendation to the same master from Général Paultre de la Mothe, then in command at Lyons, who had shown a kindly interest in the young art students. But falling in with a brother-student, Joseph Guichard (now Professor at the School of Art in Lyons), they learnt that whereas he too had started with introductions to Hersent, he had been so impressed with the superior merits of Ingres, whose pictures he had seen in the Salon, that he had transferred himself to that master's instructions. Hippolyte was impressed by his friend's arguments, and partly from a real conviction that Ingres was the superior artist, partly from the natural inclination to have the companionship of a compatriot whom he liked, he gave up the idea of seeking Hersent, and resolved to become a pupil of Ingres.

Writing to his father (April 14, 1829), Flandrin assures him that this change of purpose did not arise from caprice. "First of all," he says, "M. Ingres is reckoned in Paris as a man of higher talent than M. Hersent; and further, his school is much better governed and quieter. He does not allow the detestable buffoonery which often makes it impossible for the best men to remain in a studio."

By the 30th of that same month the brothers were established in M. Ingres' studio, and from that moment

Hippolyte Flandrin became a devoted friend and admirer of one whom he loved as a man and admired as an artist. Flandrin had to make almost a fresh start, for Ingres' views and practice in art were very different from those of Révoil; but he was not self-conceited or bent upon his own ideas, and he soon gave up all his old aspirations to become a painter of battle-fields or the like, and threw himself heart and soul into the higher art-tone of his new master. That it was more his natural element than the one into which circumstances had originally thrown him is proved alike by his works and his character, which, even in the early days of his studentship, impressed those he mixed with by its calm earnestness,—the farthest removed from what was, and probably is, too frequently the tone of the young artist-world. Throughout his life affection and respect seemed to surround Flandrin wherever he was known, his gentleness and modesty exercising a marked influence even over those who might hardly have been supposed likely to appreciate them.

"Those who knew Flandrin in his student days," says his friend, the Vicomte Delaborde, "remember a young man with a gentle, dreamy expression of almost mystic character; invariably reserved in words, and altogether stamped with such a modest nobility of mind and manner, that one felt at once, after a fashion, overawed by his modesty and attracted by his sweetness. It was the same kind of influence which he exercised a little later at Rome on all around him, to which a remarkable testimony was borne in her own way by a woman of the lower orders, who spent her life as a model to the students of the Academy. One day this woman was giving vent to a string of epigrammatic sayings, vivid and glowing as her southern skies, and dealing out slender mercies upon the personal appearance and manners of the students,—the ugliness of one, the affectation or dandyism of another, and so forth; when some one asked why she bestowed no criticism on Flandrin, who possessed neither regularity of feature nor any other definite personal beauty? There was no hesitation in her reply: "O in quanto a lui, pare proprio la Madonna!"

Such critics are apt to be truthful, and Flandrin's life did not belie the Italian peasant's notion, that "handsome or ugly, he was Madonna-like in purity and truth." The young artist who could find solace, in his life of struggle and privation in a Parisian garret, from the thought that the home circle he loved was praying for him amid those struggles; whose heart overflowed in love for his parents in expressions simple as those of a little child, notwithstanding the reserve his *habitués* remarked in him, and who remained faithful to his religious duties amid all the temptations of an artist's career in Paris, might well have carried an exterior stamp, separating him from most of his contemporaries in the keen sight of one better versed in men's ways than in books. If there were more artists in whom such a resemblance could be traced, perhaps we should have more pictures of a high standard of religious art than we actually find.

Flandrin speedily attached himself to his master with a profound admiration and respect, both as an artist and a man. Ingres' veneration for the antique, and his real science, satisfied Flandrin's taste, while his abhorrence of all that is merely factitious or conventional, and his earnest desire to promote the study of nature, and to express and characterise her truths in all their beauty and reality, satisfied the innate truthfulness and simplicity of his heart. "When you fail in the respect you owe to nature, or affect to correct her, you strike a blow at your mother herself," Ingres used to say to his pupils;[1] and it was an argument which Flandrin above all was prepared to admit.

"The empire exercised over the young artists who crowded his studio," says Vicomte Delaborde, "is a fact too well known, and established by the amount of talent brought to light beneath that powerful influence,

[1] "Quand vous manquez au respect que vous devez à la nature, quand vous prétendez la corriger, vous donnez un coup de pied dans le ventre de votre mère."

to need discussion. And to say that Flandrin received a decisive impulse from the chief's hand, is only to reaffirm what everybody knows, and what the disciple, when himself a master, acknowledged more heartily and sincerely than any one. We only need draw attention to the important element in the results which sprang from the individual qualities of the pupil. Faithful as Flandrin ever was to the teaching and example of the great artist, whose chief disciple he would scarcely have presumed to think himself, he was no less faithful to his own bent, no less ready to listen dutifully to the inner voice which guided him. While looking upon himself, (as he did in all good faith to the end,) as absolutely formed by M. Ingres, he might duly have attributed some of his individual merits, revealed as they are on canvas or wall, in a striking combination of science and inspiration, to the resources of his own imagination, and the natural elevation of his own mind. And while Flandrin was as yet occupied only in trying his strength under the master's eye, seeking progress in the strictest obedience at his work, in the most scrupulous abnegation, somewhat of that depth of tender feeling and grace, which were later to shine forth so prominently, already appeared. For the moment his business was only to paint studies from life, simple academical studies, in which the main point seemed to be the imitation of nature, according to the rules laid down by Ingres. And accordingly all Flandrin's efforts were devoted to this end, such works of his earliest years as we possess proving the attention and precision with which he applied the precepts he received to a due rendering of the realities before him. But this proves too that he was endowed with more than a most rare faculty of assimilation. If Flandrin was foremost among his fellow-students in skill and acquired science, he was no less foremost in the natural serenity of his style and the instinctive grace of his imagination. Any one who will examine the picture (in the École des Beaux Arts) which won the Roman prize, will find a sure promise of the success which ensued. Notwithstanding the difference of subject and the local conditions in either case, we may fairly affirm that those qualities which are fully developed on the walls of Saint Germain des Prés, Saint Vincent de Paul, and Saint Paul at Nîmes, may be found in germ in that pagan subject, the Recognition of Theseus."[1]

This picture was painted during a time of no small struggle and difficulty. Ingres wished his pupils to be admitted into the Academy, and in the September following their arrival in Paris we find Hippolyte writing for their baptismal registers, and announcing to

[1] *Lettres, etc. d'Hippolyte Flandrin*, p. 23.

his parents that he and his brother had been admitted to the "Concours de l'Académie."

"We have begun the competition to-day," he writes (September 14, 1829). "There are three hundred competitors, and out of these fifty have to be selected. When judgment is given, I will tell you whether we are accepted, and where we come in the list. Our school has just distinguished itself in the competition for the Roman fellowship, in the person of Étex *aîné*, who got the second sculptor's prize, and richly deserved the first, but it was taken into consideration that his rival was twenty-nine, and could not compete again. But, notwithstanding, he must be well satisfied, for M. Ingres presented him to us saying, 'Here is the *premier grand prix* for sculpture,—he richly deserves it.' One must feel very happy to receive such approbation from one's master. M. Ingres has already talked of this *concours* to me, and possibly next year I may try for it, but it is a difficult thing! Only think:—one must first compete for what is called *l'esquisse*, a composition painted from some historical subject given by the professors; then, if one is accepted, one has to paint an *académie*, and after all the trials ten men are admitted to compete for the great prize. He who is so lucky as to win it gets eight hundred francs for his journey from Paris to Rome, and an allowance of a thousand crowns for five years. Oh! if one might but be so happy!"

Eventually Flandrin attained this desired object, but for the present he was contented with a minor though very important success. On October 10, 1829, he writes home to say, "The result of the *concours* for the Académie Royale is, that out of four hundred competitors one hundred and fourteen have been accepted, ourselves being of the number. We were among the first, for I am ninth and Paul thirteenth. The difference between Paul and me is owing to some trifling thing more or less, for we are much alike as to our powers." . . .

Ingres was pleased at the success of his pupils, and having obtained a hint through a friend of the exceeding straitness of their means, he sent for Hippolyte, "spoke very encouragingly, and said he should henceforth give us twenty francs a month, half the cost of his lessons. Only think how I thanked him! But he bade me tell no one, or he should be very angry. . . . I can't, however, resist the temptation of giving you this pleasure."

Strait indeed those means were. That winter—1829-30—was exceptionally severe: the Seine was frozen over, and on all sides there was intense suffering, with which the efforts of active charity were unable fully to cope. Many persons died of the cold, and in the young Flandrins' garret the thermometer stood at 14° centigrade. They could not keep water there from freezing, and the oil in their lamp froze to a block; but Hippolyte sends a cheerful report that he and Paul "are well, and wait patiently for spring to bring a change from this severe weather."

Not unfrequently, however, the brothers had no resource save to go supperless to bed, and continually during that long hard winter they used to do this as early as five in the afternoon, as the only way of enduring the cold of their draughty, fireless attic. Sometimes indeed they were so fortunate as to have some little commission,—a sketch, or a lithograph to execute for a shop, in which case the well-husbanded oil had to be melted for their little lamp, and the pleasure of work and the food it supplied kept their blood warm; while often it involved a nice calculation as to whether they might prudently use a little of the aforesaid precious oil on anything save work, and if the decision was affirmative, the long hours spent in bed were beguiled with books, the brothers reading aloud in alternation, trying at once to forget their present discomfort, and to make up for past deficiencies in their education. It was to these studies, which were still more earnestly and methodically prosecuted later on at Rome, that Flandrin was indebted for almost everything he knew, exclusive of art. "Tardy as this self-education may have been, and incomplete in many ways," (writes Vicomte Delaborde,) "it nevertheless resulted in a reality and depth on certain subjects which are not always attained by several years' routine at college. Unquestionably with Flandrin, as with most other eminent artists, there were natural instincts capable of originating, fertile and elastic in the regions of imagination; but study and reflection had greatly added to the power of these innate capacities, and developed what began by a mere general perception and feeling into a rare delicacy and taste. I doubt," (the same eminently artistic literary man goes on to say,) "whether it be possible to fathom the mysteries of Dante's depth of thought with more penetration than did Flandrin; or whether any professor of literature ever appreciated the incomparable beauties of the Divina Commedia more truly than he did. Not to speak of Holy Scripture, with which he daily fed alike his art inspirations and his Christian faith, his memory was so well stored with the poetry of ancient times, (which he had begun to know at the age when most men forget them,) that those strains became a standing measure to which everything else was compared in his mind, and which was to him the test of false and true poetry—of real imagination or its mere imitation. Yet Flandrin could not read either Homer or Virgil in the original text, and it was only by means of translations that he could unlock the door of classic literature. But what matter, so long as by even this sidelong approach his instincts attained the object which so many who tread the direct road fail to reach? Many a scholar who is familiar with every shade of meaning in the ancient classic languages, many an adept in all imaginable grammatical difficulties, knows much less as to the general character and the moral signification of the masterpieces he has studied, than a gifted artist who has only contemplated them, so to say, at a distance through translations."

This power of pure and classic imagination was displayed in Flandrin's first real picture—his Theseus, which won him the greatly longed-for Roman scholarship. It conveys a clear idea of the struggle which the young painter was undergoing with poverty, that just before the time when this all-important *concours* was to begin, he was so entirely without money to meet the necessary expenses of colours, models, etc., that he reluctantly decided to withdraw from the competition, and it was only on hearing M. Ingres' expression of disappointment, (for he was confident in his pupil's powers, and fully believed he would prove successful,) that Flandrin resolved to face the difficulty, however great, and to endure any amount of privation and personal discomfort rather than thwart or disappoint the master for whom he felt such unbounded gratitude. But the daily struggle for subsistence was hard; a few lithographs executed on commission, an occasional copy from some great picture in the Louvre; sometimes such a piece of good luck as the portrait of a certain gendarme, who was so delighted with his own likeness that he voluntarily added five more to the stipulated price of thirty francs;—it was by such means as these that Flandrin held on for the bare life. His letters during that hard first year in Paris are full of character, bright, cheerful, and humble.

"*March* 11, 1830.

"I have not been more fortunate here, for just as the *concours* of perspective came on (which is the preliminary of others, specially that for the Roman prize, for which I had been carefully preparing and hoping to succeed in it) I fell ill, and on the very eve got a sort of *coup de sang* and feverish attack. On the day of competition I made a great effort to get up and go to the Academy. I began, but by the middle of the day I was so knocked up, I was obliged to leave off. Happily my illness did not last long, but yielded after a few days to the effects of an infusion of *millepertuis*. As to the *concours*, a great many of the young men who are fit competitors for the great prize have not studied perspective, and according to the rules they and I alike ought to be out of the competition. But this would make the class so weak, that for once the rules are to be ignored, and in this case I shall try to go in for the great *concours*."

"*April* 5, 1830.

"Dearest Mother,—It is so long since I have had the happiness of a chat with you, you must be scolding me for being so long about it; but forgive me, for latterly in particular I have had so much to do! There are all my usual studies, and others necessary for the five or six *concours* coming on, some of which have already begun; and then there is all this bother about the conscription, which keeps me running about hither and thither. Indeed that has made me terribly anxious, but I have been rather easier about it the last few days, although nothing is as yet decided. I write under cover to cousin Mariette. . . . Tell her that I have not forgotten her advice, but follow it daily. Yes, indeed, dear mother and cousin, you will see us come back to Lyons as we went, believing in God, and taking some pains to keep His Commandments. (You will be surprised that I should say believing in God, but hardly any one here does believe in Him.) We shall return loving and respecting our parents. Ah, indeed! every time I think of seeing you again I am so happy I could cry for joy. I picture to myself my arrival; how I shall run up the stairs, my heart beating fast, and then seeing you and feeling your arms round me! Then I fancy how I shall run over all the rooms with Paul;—but there is one which makes me very sad—I mean our sister's room, the sister[1] whom I do not want to make you forget; she was too good, and we shall ever have her present to our thoughts; but I want to supply her loss to you, and all our efforts shall be put forth to show you how much we love you.

"Pray let me have an answer to this letter, I want so much to know how you all are. . . . Mama, papa only writes letters of half a sheet now. I know how it tries him, but his children cannot see him any longer, and he must think of the delight it is to read his letters! As to Auguste, I expect him to write very soon. He may write what he will, if only it be a good long letter. . . . Be at rest as to our Easter duties, we are preparing for them. Five months more before we shall see you, it seems so long! But we will make good use of the time."

The following letter alludes to Flandrin's fear of being taken by the conscription:—

"*April* 15, 1830.

"My dear Papa,—At last I am out of danger, and I

[1] Caroline Flandrin, who died the end of August 1829, after a long illness.

lose no time in telling you. Yesterday I passed the Council of Revision. I had been terribly anxious since you told me my number. Nobody gave me any hope, and I should probably have been taken but for the exertions of a member of the Council to whom M. de Châteaugiron had introduced me, for one of the generals said 'There are fellows who squint worse than that sent off!'[1] But meanwhile M. de Châteaugiron's friend whispered something to the President, who shortly after dismissed me. My first thought was of the happiness it would be to you dear papa and mama; then I dressed quickly that I might run and tell Paul, who was waiting impatiently for news. So at last I am free from this anxiety, and I shall set to work with a clearer mind. . . . Something happened on Easter Day which gave me great pleasure, as I am sure it will you. I had been competing with all the other Academy pupils for the historical composition prize. The picture is done in one day, each competitor shut up in his stall. The subject was mythological; Hercules having gone down to chain Cerberus, who takes refuge under Pluto's throne, he drags the monster out by force. I did my best with it. On Easter Day, M. Ingres summoned all the competitors, and when we arrived, he expressed himself well satisfied with the competition; and then coming up to me,

[1] Flandrin had squinted from his birth.

said, 'Here is the fellow who deserved the medal, but they have been horribly unjust! You had seven votes, and the other man eleven. It has hurt me very much, and made me quite ill, for any injury done to you is as to my own children.' Then I told him what I really felt, that I greatly preferred his approbation to the medal, (which is quite true, though it is a gold medal of the first class,) and how much I feel all the trouble he takes on our behalf. He encouraged us, and urged us to do well in the three approaching *concours*, which lead on to the Roman prize, but as to that I have no hope at all. It becomes harder and harder. All the same I will tell you the results as they happen. In the last competition for places Paul was fifth. He could hardly have done better. M. Ingres is very well satisfied with us."

"PARIS, *May* 19, 1830.

"My dear Papa,—You remember the *concours* which are the steps towards competing for the Roman prize. You know that I got in at the first trial, but since that I have competed with sixty other pupils drafted out of several lots. We had to make a composition on a subject from Grecian history in one day, and each man shut up in his stall. Twenty were to be taken out of the sixty competitors, and I was the eleventh, greatly to M. Ingres' satisfaction and my own, as I thought of the pleasure it would be to you—father, mother, and brother. But I have another trial to pass, to compete with the nineteen accepted with me, and this time the subject is a great 'Academy' painted in four sittings. I began to-day, but I tremble, because I have a very bad position.[1] However, I shall do my best, and then God's Will be done."

"PARIS, *May* 31, 1830.

"My dear Papa,—The *concours* has not turned out well for me, I have not succeeded. I did worse than usual just when I ought to have done better. M. Ingres was very much vexed, yet he was very kind in comforting me, and in pointing out that next year I might be more successful in what I tried to do now. Oh, I am not at all out of heart. I burn with the love of my work, and M. Ingres! M. Ingres himself is satisfied with us. Then too we shall soon have the happiness of seeing you again, earlier than we expected, in September I think. The very thought fills me with a kind of impatience and joy such as I never felt before! How delightful it will be!"

Soon after the Revolution of July 1830 broke out, and Flandrin's next letters are brief, their object being merely to allay the anxieties his parents were sure to feel on behalf of himself and his brother Paul.

[1] In the hall where the competitors painted.

"*July* 28, 1830.

"Fearing you will be alarmed about us when you hear of the outbreak here, I write to assure you that we are keeping quietly at home, and acting very prudently. We hear perpetual firing, everybody is taking arms and making ready for the worst. The Palais Royal quarter, boulevards and quays, are the scene of battle. It is very sad. What will come of it all? But grievous and horrible as it is, pray, dearest father and mother, do not be anxious about us; we will not go out. I only beg Auguste to be as prudent at Lyons as we are here. . . . I cannot frank my letter, the street is intersected by barricades, but please be easy, we will not run into danger. Write to us."

Shortly after this the brothers went home, making the long journey on foot, and returning in October to Paris in the same primitive way.

On October 26, 1830, Hippolyte writes:—"We came by Arnay-le-Duc, Saulieu, Avallon, Vermanton, etc., walking fourteen or fifteen *lieues* daily. At Auxerre we found the Garde Nationale of several towns called out. It seems some days ago the labourers and vinedressers of Auxerre combined to demand that the price of corn be lowered, and they gathered round the Hôtel de la Préfecture with loud threats. The Garde Nationale tried to disperse them, but the mob disarmed and ill-used several, and burnt warehouses, broke into stores, and sold the corn as they pleased. So further help was called in, and the Garde Nationale from several places round came to disperse the mob, and made a good many prisoners. Further on we came upon some hussars who were going to support the National Guard. Otherwise our journey was uneventful. I never was hotter or saw finer weather, which lasted us to Paris,—and it is more noisy and lively than ever."

Flandrin's eldest brother Auguste had followed the family bent, and was likewise an artist; but under the pressure of poverty he was at present disposed to devote himself entirely to the more certainly remunerative work of lithography. Hippolyte wished his brother to come forth into a more artistic sphere; and eventually Auguste yielded to his advice, and came also to Paris to study under Ingres. The following letter is on this subject:—

"PARIS, *Nov.* 1, 1830.

"My good and dear Auguste,—I write to tell you something which has pleased us very much, when we went to see M. Ingres on our return. He received us warmly, embraced us several times, and then we showed him the sketches made at Lyons. He was very much pleased with them, first of all with those from the Perugino,[1] and then those made during our journey, among which he picked out the Quay of Saint Clair and the views of Bugey. Among these he greatly admired the coloured sketch of the Forest of Mazières, with the Lake of Geneva in the distance, and said it was admirable, but the Pyramion, half-covered with clouds, fixed his attention. He took it aside to examine it, and then exclaimed, 'Your brother must have a great deal of talent!' He told me to make a foreground, whatever I pleased; and then to keep it, as he would use it as a background in one of his pictures. He thinks it would be a great pity if you do not paint, and I entreat you with all my heart to do so. I believe you would sell your pictures, and I know you would be happy in the occupation,—only choose fine subjects such as raise your own mind. Draw scenes in which nature is great and terrible, such as the valleys of Saint Rambert or Charabottes, or the hills of Ain. How I enjoy recalling them! and we were together then!

". . . Now to answer you as to my mind and Paul's as to Gros's pictures. We do not like them, because, to say nothing of the drawing, which is very weak, they are devoid of power and effect. There is plenty to catch the eye of what is glittering and brilliant, but that is all. I grant that there is very skilful

[1] The Ascension in the Museum at Lyons.

manipulation in his pictures, but it is not what one wants, for it is not a good rendering of nature, which is far more tranquil. We may be told that we are cold, but, on the contrary, the nature that I behold is far warmer, more vigorous and energetic than Gros paints it, but at the same time it is calmer. This is what I think, but do not let what I say go beyond our own home."

"PARIS, *Dec.* 17, 1830.

"My dear Papa,— . . . We are well, except that I have had bad toothache for the last month, and have at last had two teeth drawn in three days. I was sorry to lose them, but I was suffering so much, and could hardly do anything. Now I am better, and we are hard at work. God grant that we may not be hindered by war, for we should most certainly be in the Garde Mobile, and no one would care to be dispensed from that. Meanwhile we are working as if nothing could interrupt us, and I believe it is the best thing to do: —one must use the present moment well if one does not wish to regret it afterwards."

"ESTRÉPAGNY, EURE, *Dec.* 28, 1830.

"My dear Papa,—I know you will be very much surprised at the date of my letter, but I will tell you how it has come to pass. The ministers' prosecution raised an excitement in Paris, and all the row went on in our quarter,[1] it being supposed that they were in the Luxembourg. It was necessary to keep troops and National Guard out (there were certainly forty thousand men in our quarter). The people were shouting for the ministers' heads, and would not wait for the judgment. Free circulation in the streets was stopped; we were obliged to be escorted by National Guards to get into our own room. One could do nothing at the studio; in short, everything looked like an immediate crisis. So, one of our companions[2] asked us to go with him to his relations in Normandy, and work with him. After asking M. Ingres' leave, we accepted, and here we are, most kindly received by his parents, who are very good to us. They live near Rouen, to which place we have just made an expedition. Some other time I will tell you about all the interesting things we have seen. We received the trunk on the day we started. Really, dear papa, we cannot thank you enough for the trouble you have taken about it and all its contents, great-coats, trousers, shoes and stockings, portfolios, cover-lids. We are most heartily grateful for all these things. We know all your love for us; we have had plenty of proofs of that all our lives, and we thank you for everything with hearts full of gratitude and love. . . ."

[1] The Flandrins were at this time occupying a room in the Rue Mazarin.

[2] Jules Bisset.

"PARIS, *Feb.* 18, 1831.

". . . Complaints in every direction! I don't know if it is the same at Lyons, but here people complain more of the new government than of the old. The newspapers cry out, and caricatures are more spiteful than ever. I don't know if there is just cause, but it seems as though it were difficult to rule, since France changes her *régime* ten times in thirty years, and is none the better satisfied. I should know but little of what goes on if others in the studio did not talk about it; I am altogether too much occupied with drawing and painting to acquire information otherwise. I do most earnestly desire to get on, in order to relieve you of the sacrifices you make for us. I work as hard as ever I can. . . . My thoughts are often full of you, and those are the pleasantest I have."

"PARIS, *March* 30, 1831.

"We are doing all we can to earn something. I have a pupil at fifteen francs a month, who comes to our room for his lessons. It is not much, but still! M. Ingres daily shows more kindly interest in us: he has just put the climax to his goodness by remitting all that we ought to pay him, so that we have nothing to spend but ten francs a month for models. We do all we can to show our gratitude, and I have been so fortunate as to be able to be of some use in making some copies for him. He encourages me to try and get into the *concours* for the Roman prize. Before that there are twenty trials, but I will make every effort, and then, whatever the result may be, I shall have nothing to reproach myself with. Our time is quite filled with studying in M. Ingres' studio, the *concours* at the Academy, and preparation for what is called the *concours de Rome.* That implies a great deal of trouble and work, for one has to hunt up museums and libraries, in order to learn about the costumes and ways of the ancients, and to read up their history. We shall know in May whether I get in, and meanwhile I am working with a hearty good will. . . . We often see M. Foyatier, and he very kindly sometimes asks us to dinner, we gladly accepting. He is working at several statues for the great exhibition about to take place. M. Ingres, our dear master and benefactor, is also going to exhibit a large and admirable picture.[1] Oh, what a good disciple I want to be !"

"PARIS, *April* 15, 1831.

" . . . Oh! how I love our dear M. Ingres, and how earnestly I long to do him credit in the *concours!* Three of these are just over, and successfully; that of perspective, of attitude, and of composition. May

[1] The Martyrdom of S. Symphorien, which was not finished till three years later.

God be pleased to help me on to the end, for I have still two *concours* to go through before reaching that which is called the *concours de Rome.* But it will all be settled soon, and I will write and tell you the result.

"There has been a fresh census made of the National Guard in Paris just lately, and I could not escape this time. I am inscribed on the lists of the Garde Mobile. I was asked if I could supply my uniform, but I answered that it was impossible, so, whenever I am wanted, I shall be clothed and equipped by the Government. What I want to get off is the service of the Garde Sédentaire, because mounting guard and exercising are such a loss of time. But when the Garde Mobile is called out you may be sure the case is urgent, and everybody ought to be willing to contribute to the safety and defence of their country, and to be ready to leave everything for so useful and honourable a duty. A few days ago we had a splendid review of forty thousand men. The King presented the standards, and the troops were magnificent, especially some of the cavalry, among others the Cuirassiers. It was a Sunday—neither muddy nor dusty—the Champ de Mars was quite full between spectators and troops, and it lasted till evening. All went off well, and no accident marred the day's success."

There is a P.S. to this letter in Paul Flandrin's handwriting as follows:—"Papa, I am quite out of breath! I rushed up to tell Hippolyte that he has got the medal, the composition prize. I have just heard it. I am so glad to have to tell you such a good thing. I can imagine your pleasure. We saw the exhibition this morning, and everybody adjudged the prize to him."

"PARIS, *May* 30, 1831.

"*Mon bon ami*, my dear Auguste,—I have got through the last trial before reaching the *concours* for the great prize, but it has been cruelly hard! The subject was a figure painted three feet high. I did it, and yesterday was the day of judgment. I was satisfied myself, I had good reason to hope; but you shall hear! M. Ingres, M. Guérin, M. Granet, and three other members of the Institut, on going into the exhibition hall, pronounced me to be first. But no, M. Gros and his party carried the day, and I was tossed out from being first to last; and finally M. Ingres, in despair, went away, after protesting with all his might against what had been done, and I was rejected! You can fancy how I felt yesterday when I heard it; that is to say, when I learnt that I had been rejected, without knowing any of the circumstances. I did not dare go near M. Ingres, and yet I had nothing to reproach myself with; my figure was much the best, I may say so without vanity. At last, in the evening, I resolved to go to him. I found him at the dinner-table, but he could not eat. Several members of the Institute, M. Guérin among them, had come to comfort him, but he was a long way off that. He received me saying, 'Here is the lamb that has been butchered!' And then, addressing his wife, who was trying to quiet him, he said, 'Oh! you have no idea how cruel and bitter injustice is to a young man's heart!' and all this was said with such a heartfelt manner, that the tears were falling from my eyes. He made me sit down to dinner, and embraced me as a father his son. I went away comforted. How much I owe to this man, who has already done so great things for us, and who has, perhaps, done most of all now. I don't know what to say to him, what to call him, but the thought of him fills my eyes with tears, out of mere gratitude. But still, from time to time I am beset with regrets, for it might have been a great start for me, and I had good reason to hope. I was prepared to strain every nerve. I was *en train*, and, moreover, it was the only way of testifying my gratitude to M. Ingres, for to you, dear brother, I may say it—my good master had reckoned greatly on my picture. Perhaps he was too hopeful, but I would have spared nothing to justify his confidence. And then it would have been such a pleasure to papa and mama, and to you. I felt all that, and it doubled the delight I felt in what I hoped. I shall keep my painting, the one just rejected, for you, and bring it to you when I come to Lyons."

There is a touching little incident connected with this picture, and the competition for which it was produced. As usual, Hippolyte was greatly straitened for means, and had he been admitted as a competitor for the Roman prize ("*admis en loge*," as the technical phrase is) he would have been unprepared to meet the inevitable though not very heavy expenses. So, feeling tolerably confident of such a prospect, he decided on the only attainable means of raising necessary funds, and wrote to his brother Auguste, in whose hands the medal he had won a month before was left, to sell it to some goldsmith, and send him the money. Auguste had a small sum in hand himself, which he forwarded at once to Hippolyte, cherishing the first token of his younger brother's success, which he could not bear to sell, and when Hippolyte, finding what had been done, wanted to return the money, which, however acceptable, had lost its original object, Auguste affectionately insisted on his brother's keeping it and using it as he pleased. Hippolyte accordingly made use of it to begin a small picture now in the possession of his family, called, "Virgil's Shepherds," which was finished later on at Rome, when the much-desired scholarship had been really won.

"PARIS, *June* 29, 1831.

"My Dear Papa,—Forgive me for not answering sooner—it was owing to something stronger than I! I have been confined to bed for some days with a malady which is very common here, called *le* or *la grippe* (influenza), and I would not write until I was getting quite well for fear of making you anxious.

"Dear father and mother, it was your fête day lately, and I let it pass unnoticed! But what could I say? That I love you? Oh, you know that! My whole heart is yours, and I can only renew the deed of gift! It is wholly yours, and will always beat fast at the precious names of father and mother. And all I can say Paul says too,—he is heartily one with me.

"I knew how keenly you would share my trouble at my failure in the examination. From time to time regrets will come over me anew, but on the whole I am comforted (which is more than I thought to be). But that you know is M. Ingres' doing,—you heard of all his kindness to me. I shall never forget it all! He often does the same sort of thing. The other day he inquired whether I thought you were vexed with me because of my failure, as, if it were so, he would write something on my behalf in one of my home letters. I told him I did not think you were vexed with me, but that all the same I should be very pleased if he would write. So he promised, and I am going to take my letter to him. . . . Mama, if you see Madame Lacuria, tell her, please, that her son is well. He took great care of me during my illness, and did all manner of things for me. Dear papa and mama, take care of yourselves, that your children may find you well, and have no drawback to the pleasure of seeing you. The time will soon come. Oh, how delicious it is to think of coming home!"

Hippolyte might say that he was too busy to know anything of the outer world on his own account, but he was too genuine a Frenchman to be without keen feeling for European politics. His enthusiasm for Poland, common to so many of his day, breaks out in some letters of this date:

"PARIS, *Aug.* 1, 1831.

". . . . Our life here is very quiet, and I have nothing to tell but what I have told you over and over again. From time to time some event rouses us, but not often. Such an exceptional thing has just happened in the recent fêtes. We saw the magnificent review which the King held on the 29th, and a glorious sight it was. There were at least a hundred and thirty thousand men under arms, two hundred cannon, and as many caissons, which altogether made two immense lines, nearly two miles long, crossing the town from barrier to barrier. The whole defiled before the King and Don Pedro, the Emperor of Brazil, shouting 'Vive la Pologne' with the utmost enthusiasm. May these shouts reach the Russian camps and their Emperor's palace, and tell them that the Poles will not be destroyed, for they kindle the sympathy of every generous heart. Oh, that Poland were not so far off!"

Before this he had written to his brother Auguste:—"*Dis donc*—it seems as if papa thought me a Carlist. I don't know what has given him the idea, but truly, I don't believe anybody loves liberty more than I do, and as a proof I like the Belgians, and I admire the Poles and their great deeds. If one admires their deeds one must needs recognise and admire the principle whence they spring. As for me, I pray daily that they may be triumphant; but one must do something more, and give them practical help. Are we to do nothing for a nation which fought side by side with our troops for fifteen years, which fell with us, and which has undergone so much barbarous mutilation and oppression merely because its cause was bound up with our own? Many people grumble, but government holds its own, and does not heed popular clamour. But all this is only for you—I say it to you, because I like you to know all I think."

The brothers had just paid another visit to their home, (again on foot,) when a serious insurrection broke out in Lyons among the always hot-headed, insubordinate silk-weavers of that city; occasioned this time by the promulgation of a fixed tariff of wages. The young Flandrins were overtaken at Sens by tidings of what had been going on, and hardly refrained from going back to be near their parents in a season of danger. However, they judged it wiser to go on to Paris, and hear the true state of things, and there tidings from home satisfied them to a certain extent that their return to Lyons was useless. But Hippolyte writes vehemently to Auguste, indignant with the Government, and ready to defend all the Lyonnese, masters and workmen alike!

The winter of 1832 was another season of laborious trial and strict self-denial. Hippolyte began for the first time to suffer from the rheumatic affections which were a continual torture to him during the rest of his life, fostered as they were by frequent work in damp or cold churches. This first attack seems to have come on while he was engaged in copying Sebastian del Piombo's Visitation in the Louvre.

"For the last month" (he writes February 14, 1832) "I have been working at the Musée at a copy. It pays badly, but then while earning something I am studying too, as the picture is a fine one. The worst of it is having to work without any fire in a gallery seven hundred feet long. The winter is not very severe, but I can tell you it needs a good will to remain five or six hours together without stirring."

Another and more imminent peril was at hand in the shape of cholera. Hippolyte writes to his father:—

"PARIS, *March* 27, 1832.

"I must send you scraps and odd bits, for I have not a clear hour to myself. The examinations are coming on, and they follow so fast one upon the other that the several studies necessary for each fill up all my time. It won't do to dawdle! Dear papa, you are afraid lest we should want for anything, but we are only afraid lest you should inconvenience yourself too much for us, and that distresses us. We have never spent so little as this winter, and that because we, with Lacuria, have cooked for ourselves. We clubbed together, bought a great saucepan and three pots, and now we make soups and dishes of potatoes, and sometimes a *pot au feu*, which lasts the whole week. You may imagine that the cooking is plain, but it is more wholesome than in a restaurant; and perhaps feeding in this way may help us to escape the cholera morbus, which has broken out here suddenly, terrifying everybody. No other subject is talked about, and the wonderful thing is that it has happened in the midst of splendid weather, which we have had for the last two months. People expected to see the cholera advance gradually through the departments between Paris and England; but not at all! it leapt straight from London here. Wards are set aside in the hospitals, ambulances, and depôts for drugs are prepared on all sides, but they say the best remedy is in an orderly, quiet, and simple habit of life. And so we try not to be fidgetty; for, according to that, we may be hopeful. Our room is clean and airy, and so we entreat you not to be anxious about us. Let us have trust in God.

"You will have heard already at Lyons that the cholera is here, and so I write without loss of time to tell you that both of us and Lacuria are well."

"PARIS, *April* 13, 1832.

"I have just received your letter, which shows how alarmed you are about us, but I think you would get one from me that same day. It was not altogether reassuring, for Paris was anything but quiet, and the ravages of the cholera were spreading. Since that it has been worse still; more than a thousand persons have been attacked daily. Indeed it is a sad sight to see all the litters carrying sick people, or processions of ten or twelve corpses at once—no rare thing, I assure you. But for the last two days the malady has visibly decreased; not only fewer people are attacked, but the disease is less severe, and more easily subdued. May God grant that it spare Lyons!"

"PARIS, *April* 19, 1832.

"My Dear Papa and Mama,—I have received your last letter which speaks of our coming to Lyons. I did not answer the same day, because Lacuria had just written to his parents on the same subject, and I thought they would give you tidings of us; so I waited two days, in order that you might hear the oftener.

"We had thought of going to Lyons in order to share your danger if the cholera reached you, but meanwhile it broke out so suddenly here that we have been so far in a state of indecision. The best doctors say, and all the newspapers repeat their opinion, that it is most imprudent to go away now. They say that if one is in the heart of the malady and has become acclimatised, it is better to stay quiet, for that one is much more likely to sicken in a change of air; and this has been pretty well proved by the number of people who, flying from Paris, have been taken ill, twenty, thirty, or forty miles hence, in places where there had been no previous infection. So you see, dear papa, that we have substantial reasons for deciding to remain.

Moreover, the worst of the evil is happily over, it is dying away, and it is quite impossible to account for the line of its advance. There were great apprehensions about the more confined and dirty quarters of Paris, but so far the cholera has not been worse there than elsewhere;—for instance, our quarter, which is certainly one of the best, has been most severely attacked. Happily it is decreasing now, and has crossed the river. It is said now to be worst in the Marais.

"The reports sent to Lyons must have been very alarming, and perhaps they may have been exaggerated. But the scourge has been very severe, for yesterday the *Moniteur* officially announced more than ten thousand deaths since the beginning. I trust that all necessary precautions will be taken at Lyons, since there at any rate there is some warning. Be as easy about us as you can. Take care of yourselves for our sakes."

In his next letters to his father Flandrin says: "We have no time to think about the cholera, for now I am embarked in the *concours*, and have gained a medal which gives me a permanent right to the first *places* in the Academy. But now the matter in hand is the famous Roman *concours*." And a few days later he says: "I told you that I had got a medal. Well, since that the whole school has competed for the historical composition. Twenty were to be selected out of this large number, and I was fifth. Now there is the last trial to come, the one in which I was rejected last year. I am preparing for it with all my might, and mean to pull hard at the collar. M. Ingres is very much pleased at the way in which I have been received. He is as kind and good to us as ever—we often go to his house. He is well, and I pray God to preserve him long to us."

All this time Flandrin's health was in a very uncertain state, and practically he was quite unfit for the work before him. Weakened as he had been by privation and overwork, the atmospheric influences of the cholera told severely upon him, and he became so weak that he could literally not walk without the support of his brother's arm; and almost immediately after the beginning of this anxious competition (his *entrée en loge*, as it is called) he became too ill for any further resistance, and had to take to his bed, in spite of the importance of the work in hand. It was a severe trial, and the more alarming that one of Flandrin's fellow-competitors for the Roman prize was struck down by the cholera, and died almost at once. The doctor who was called in to Flandrin threatened him with the like results if he attempted to leave his bed, still more if he tried to work; and for a few days he submitted, from sheer impossibility of doing anything else. But the moment he felt the least return of strength he dragged his weary frame back to the scene of competition, leaning painfully on his brother's arm; and after working till he well-nigh dropped, he would go back to bed for the next day, quite exhausted, to begin the same process the day after! Perhaps the excitement really kept him up—anyhow, with his usual affectionate consideration for his parents, Hippolyte treated his illness as lightly as possible to them. He writes:—

"DE MA LOGE, PARIS, *June* 1, 1832.

"I write a hasty line because you are anxious and believe me to be ill. I did not know that Lacuria had said anything about it, or I would have given you particulars before. It is only that I have had just a little touch of cholera. It lasted five days, during which I was pretty well spent, but the cousin of one of my companions nursed me, and I soon got well. Happily it was not much, and now I am full of very different matters! I have to paint a picture, it is my first, and I am competing with men who have tried seven or eight times already. But I will not be discouraged,—at least I hope I shall not."

"PARIS, *June* 24, 1832.

"I wish I could see you, . . . but I am forcibly detained here—gratitude itself ties me down. I must try to justify M. Ingres' confidence by my picture, I must defend his doctrine and the credit of his school against men who are so prejudiced, that even if they saw the truth they would not acknowledge it for fear of condemning themselves. You see I have a weighty task upon my shoulders; God grant that I may be able to bear it. But if it should crush me, at least I shall have left nothing undone, and shall have used every effort."

"PARIS, *Aug.* 31, 1832.

"At last I can give you a sign of life. Thank God I have come to an end of the *concours*. Now there is a month to wait before knowing the result, which is trying, as we should already have set out to join you, if I did not fear that M. Ingres, who takes so much interest in us, might think us indifferent. So we must wait till after the judgment, which will be given by the end of September. Till then our pictures are all under seal, and M. Ingres—whose first glance will pronounce my sentence—will only see mine at the same time with the rest of the jury. I await that with the keenest impatience, for one word of praise from him is of infinite value to me. On the last day of competition the candidates can communicate with one another, so that we saw each other's pictures. Mine is in quite a different line from the rest, and it made an impression which they did not conceal. They judged me much more favourably than I have judged myself, for they talked about my winning the prize, and I was not thinking of that. The Director, Sub-director, and Professor who came that evening to affix the seal of the School on the pictures, spoke of mine to M. Ingres, and very favourably too. All this would tend to excite my hopes, but no! I must keep them down. My dear master is on tenterhooks like myself. He often says, 'Oh, if you have done well how much I shall owe to you!' How dreadfully long this month will seem!"

"PARIS, *Sept.* 9, 1832.

"My dear Auguste,—If you only knew how impatient we are to see you! But various essential matters hinder me, things which I cannot set aside. I am waiting most impatiently for the time when M. Ingres will be able to tell me what he thinks of my picture. You can hardly imagine how I long for and yet dread the moment! The judgment of my competitors was in its favour, and I must confess to you that in my own heart and conscience I think myself superior to the rest. This is a confession which I entreat you to keep to yourself—it might appear unseemly for me to make it. Besides, I warn you that I expect nothing;

for my work is not in the least like the present style of things. Not that I am the least bit satisfied with my picture anyhow—I see numbers of faults which with more time I could have corrected; but remember that there are twelve figures, background, a great deal of architecture, and a heap of accessories: and all that had to be done in thirty-five days, for I was ill during the first six weeks, and the others had half done before I began to paint."

At last the longed-for moment arrived, and Flandrin found he had been successful! Let him tell his own story.

"PARIS, *Sept.* 25, 1832.

"My dear Papa and Mama,—I must tell you of our joy. I have worked hard and taken great trouble, but I am altogether rewarded by the satisfaction of my dear master. Let me tell you everything. To-day our pictures were exhibited. When the time of opening drew near my heart beat fast, for it is very alarming to find oneself for the first time exposed to public criticism and censure. At last the doors were opened, the public entered, and from behind I could look on at the groups of spectators. First I saw an enormous gathering cluster round my picture, and then a number of people whom I did not know asked me if I was not M. Flandrin? and when I said yes, they congratulated me. A minute after all our own fellow-students arrived together. They examined, criticised, and then came up to me, squeezed me, surrounded me, embraced me; and indeed these tokens of friendship pleased me very much! Soon after the men from other studios came, and many of them added their testimony to that of my own comrades; and then there came a crowd of people whom I had never seen, among whom were some of the reporters, as you may see in the *Constitutionnel* of the 26th. I was very happy in the general approbation, but I still wanted that of M. Ingres; he had not yet seen my picture, and I trembled. About noon I went to see him, and told him what was going on at the Exhibition. He shed tears of joy, and told me to come back at five o'clock, when he should have seen it. All the day there was a crowd round my picture. When five o'clock came I went to my master. He met me with open arms, and told me that very few painters had made so brilliant a *débût*, that he was proud of me as his pupil, and a number of other flattering things. I repeat all this because you are my father, mother and brother, and because what gladdens me makes you so happy. And certainly I could not have a more welcome reward than M. Ingres' satisfaction, and the way in which he expressed it. In short, the day's result is, that artists and the public have decided by an immense majority that I deserve the prize. With the public and M. Ingres on my side I think that I *do* deserve it, but I don't expect to get it."

"*Thursday, 27th.*—To-day the crowd is as great as yesterday, and says the same thing. Many people have been to congratulate M. Ingres, which pleases him very much. This morning he went to his pupils, and praised my picture highly, speaking of us with so much kindness and affection. All this is far more than I expected."

"*Friday, 28th.*—There is still a crowd around my picture, and everybody says I shall get the prize; but I don't believe it, for the cabal is horribly active.

"Here we are at Saturday, 29th. It is the day of judgment, but yet I am much calmer than when I was waiting for M. Ingres' opinion. Now he and the public have adjudged the prize to me, and that makes me calm. I have done my best, and I hope I shall bear injustice bravely since I have done my duty. Among painters our battle is the struggle between good and evil—the two principles can never be reconciled; and so our enemies are going to collect all their strength. M. Ingres has just left me to go to the judgment, saying, 'We shall see how far men can carry iniquity!'" Below the last lines come the following words, written with a trembling hand in large writing:—"Well, I was mistaken! I have got the prize! I will tell you all fully soon. Adieu! Your son who loves you, oh, so very much!"

"PARIS, *Sept.* 30, 1832.

"My dear Papa and Mama,—You cannot fancy M. Ingres' delight! In spite of all his enemies one of his pupils has at last succeeded in winning this prize! To be the French student sent to Rome, and that by universal consent! My picture remains at the school, to be placed in the *Salle des grands prix.*

"Our journey will be delayed still, for the prizes are not given yet, and I must receive my brevet with my own hand. I am very sorry, for I long to embrace you, tell and explain everything to you; but we must wait another three weeks. It does seem so long!

"An idea has come into our head, and if it could come to pass I should be so delighted! It is, that Auguste might come at once to Paris; he would see the distribution of prizes, the Exhibition, in short, all Paris; and after a few days we should set out together for Lyons, and after staying there for two months I should start for Rome, where I must be by January 1st. If Auguste could do this, it would make me very happy; but he must make haste, for we long to get to you.

"M. Ingres is always talking to me of Rome, and what I am to do there. It seems that I shall inhabit the Villa Medici, the most beautiful palace in Rome, that city of palaces. I cannot realise it! What a wonderful thing, to have five years entirely given up to study and cultivating one's talent! On the other hand, there are some very sad things. M. Ingres says that next year Paul must get the first prize for landscape, but meanwhile we shall be separated. Think of that!"

"PARIS, *Oct.* 21, 1832.

"My dear Papa,—I am still kept from you, first by a portrait I am painting for M. Ingres which I cannot get finished, and further, by what does not depend on myself. I have to receive my passport for Rome, and the money for my journey, all which is done at the Ministère des Affaires Étrangères, where they do not hurry themselves. But they have been promised me this week, and then I shall take leave of my dear master and come to you quickly. . . .

"Now for a piece of news! Paul has competed for the first time in historical landscape composition. Yesterday judgment was given, and it is he, it is Paul has won the medal! We *are* pleased, and so is M. Ingres; he looks upon it as a good augury for the great prize next year. Long live M. Ingres and his school!

"The distribution of prizes came off a few days ago at the Institut. People say that there never was such applause as burst out when I went up to salute the President and M. Ingres. My dear good master was so moved, and squeezed me in his arms so tightly! How I do love him! more than I can tell. I hope soon to tell you the day we start, and the day we shall arrive. I am boiling with impatience. Adieu! I embrace you all three with my whole heart."

Flandrin was the first pupil of Ingres who had won the *grand prix*, and it was an event which caused a great stir in the art world of Paris. "The success of his school," says Vicomte Delaborde, "had the charm of novelty to some, but to others it signified a double victory over the old academic idealism, and over the avowedly revolutionary tone which inspired a certain set of artists at that time."

All this contributed to make Flandrin a greater fame than was usual under the circumstances, and he found himself suddenly becoming a celebrity, less on account of his real talent than as the advanced guard or representative of a party. This was not, however, the temptation it might have been to a more vain or self-conscious man; he was never disposed to come forward or meet the world's advances, and even if his natural humility and simplicity had not withheld him from profiting by the opening society offered him, his means were an effectual barrier between the young artist and such indulgence. He could not even afford the clothes necessary; and when M. Bertin, director of the *Journal des Débats* (a man of considerable weight in the political and literary world), wishing to make acquaintance with the rising artist, invited him to dinner, Flandrin had to find some excuse, his real reason for not accepting being scarcely available, *i.e.* that he possessed nothing in the way of head gear save a *casquette,* and had not wherewithal to buy a hat.

Six happy weeks were spent by Flandrin at Lyons with his family, and then at last he set off for the Paradise of artists—Rome, accompanied by two other successful competitors for the *grand prix;* Léveil, who had won that for architecture, and Ambroise Thomas, the future composer of *Caïd* and the *Songe d'une nuit d'été,* who had just gained the first prize for musical composition, and to whom, from this time, Flandrin was bound with the ties of closest friendship. From Thomas, Flandrin learnt what music really is, and during the happy days spent in the Villa Medici, it was the young painter's constant delight, after a day of hard study and work, to spend the evening listening to his friend's exquisite rendering of the *chefs-d'œuvre* of his art. It was a delight which never failed to the end; until the day when the same skilled and loving hands for the last time drew forth from the organ of Saint Germain des Prés the strains to which his friend's ear was closed for ever in this life; and while Hippolyte Flandrin's coffin waited before the altar, Ambroise Thomas burst forth with Beethoven's great Andante (Symphony in A), and almost overwhelmed himself by the memories and associations wakened thereby.

To those now accustomed to rush through the great Mont Cenis tunnel, the following account of the young artist's journey will seem almost like fiction.

"ROME, *Jan.* 12, 1833.

"My dear Papa and Mama,—I must set you at rest and tell you of our journey and safe arrival. After I had said good-bye to you and my brothers, those dear brothers! I felt that I was really rushing away from you and from Lyons. As long as I could I looked back to Lyons, which contains all I love, and sighed heavily. One of my companions did all in his power to cheer me, but he did not set to work the right way. His gaiety worried me, tears would have relieved me far more than laughing and singing. However, by degrees they brightened me up, and the first night we slept at La Tour du Pin. . . . The next day we entered Savoy—inspection by the Savoyard Douane, and approach to the Alps. I enjoyed my companions' admiration, for they had never seen anything of the kind, and I shared it heartily, for the scenery was very fine. We entered a very narrow valley, frowning rocks above us, the road cut out of their sides, and down below the precipice a torrent, the foam of which we could see as we heard its roar. The weather was fine, but the temperature grew colder, and in a few hours we began to walk over snow (I say walk, for we constantly did walk, and that very willingly). The next day we crossed the Grotte des Échelles, and went for some hours through a wild valley, which however grew wider as we approached Chambéry, which is a pretty, lively town, and all around it cheerful. Montmélian and Aiguebelle are in this valley, and then we entered into the Maurienne. There the landscape changes, it becomes wilder, the pyramid-like mountains are of darker rocks, scattered over with fir-trees, whose dark boughs add to the gloom of the scene. The valley rises up to Lanslebourg, and you see Mont Cenis. At three o'clock in the morning we began the ascent. Our team consisted of eight mules and seven *conducteurs*. We went slowly, by the light of a lantern : —everything was covered with snow, nothing to be heard but the *grelots* of our team, and the howling wind, which soon brought the clouds over us, so that we could see no farther than the ground we stood on. A fine snow came whirling round and blinded us ; and meanwhile we listened to a story told by one of the men, of a post carriage which went over the precipice ten days ago. Everything was lost, men, horses and carriage. He wound up by saying, 'As for to-day I am not afraid of the snow, but it is the wind!' And then the coachman, the one you saw, asked very gravely if we had said our prayers, and commended his wife and children to God. All this was not exactly alarming, but it was rather exciting. We three young men went on ahead, and were first at the top. We could see nothing but the road, the clouds, the crosses put up here and there to mark the windings of the way, and the little refuges. At the top we breakfasted; the mules were taken off, and we went on with our three horses. And now our troubles began; for, crossing the plain of Mont Cenis, there was a high wind, the carriage got into ruts, and we had to keep it from upsetting by pulling it with ropes on the opposite side from that on which it was tilted. I can assure you I never was hotter than while about this, knee-deep in the snow! Part of the descent on the Italian side was difficult, but we soon left the snow, the sun grew warm, the mountains were lower, and we reached Susa in splendid weather, and so went on to Turin.

"We stayed a day at Turin, and I wrote to you from there. The streets are straight, wide, and full of life. The two next days we were in the plains of Lombardy. At the Austrian customhouses we were examined and rummaged, and even the letters in our portfolios were read. At last we arrived at Milan, a superb town which one should have plenty of time to see. We spent Christmas Day and the following day there. The cathedral is sublime, all in white marble, more than three hundred and sixty feet high; we went up to the top twice by an open staircase. The interior is full of precious sculptures and pictures, in short, the whole thing is a marvel. It is impossible to tell you all we saw in a letter, but we made careful notes each evening, and I shall lose nothing.

"After Milan, we saw Piacenza, Parma, Modena. Everywhere customhouses, everywhere passports called for, coming in and going out of all the towns—it is a downright persecution. Many a time we cried out *Vive la France!* We stayed a day at Bologna, and then started again to cross the Apennines. At first we had bad weather in the mountains; there was a fine snow falling all that day and the next morning, but about nine o'clock the wind rose, carried away the mists, and gave us a view of the mountains. The road became worse and worse, and we were constantly obliged to have four oxen as a *renfort* to our three horses. The summits of the Apennines are wild, and the crosses one sees here and there are dreary, for they are expiatory, and point out the spot of some assassination. We were ascending still for three-quarters of this day. The wind was terrible; it carried the snow about like dust, and we were constantly smothered in whirlwinds of it. The clouds rested on the mountain crests, and were carried away with frightful rapidity. More than once we thought the carriage would be upset, but happily we got over all the highest points without accident, which is more than every one can say, for we saw one carriage upset. At last the weather became glorious, and the next day we descended and reached Florence. I must jump over the rest of our journey, which was prosperous, and tell you about Rome.

"We saw it, not without excitement, when about five *lieues* off; the dome of St. Peter's rising above all. A few minutes after we met some of our comrades, who had come to meet us; all the others had made a mistake, and come out the day before. At the Porta del Popolo I met M. Bodinier's brother,[1] and several other friends who went with us to the Academy. We were delightfully received by the students, and dined that evening with M. Horace Vernet. As the student whom I succeed is ill, I have a charming room provisionally. I command the whole town; and the first thing I saw from my bed on waking was St. Peter's and the Vatican. The house and gardens and everything is far better than I had been told. Why are

[1] Bodinier is a French artist, the painter of various Italian subjects, among which a picture called "Ave Maria dans la Campagne de Rome" is well known. It is now in the Museum at Angers.

you not here, in this glorious country? The next day, at breakfast, I got M. Ingres' letter enclosed in yours. Oh ! what a pleasure it was, I kissed them, and cried over them. . . ."

Flandrin's delight in Rome was as great as might be expected. In his first letter to his brothers he speaks enthusiastically of his visit to the Vatican, which had exceeded his greatest expectations. Especially he particularises the Mass of Bolsena,[1] the School of Athens and the Dispute. He writes to his parents:—

"ROME, *Feb.* 6, 1833.

"Rome comprises everything necessary to make an artist happy; a glorious sky, a beautiful country, a fine type of men, grand monuments, and the most splendid pictures and sculptures. Every day I make acquaintance with some *chef-d'œuvre*, but I do not hurry, because one grows utterly weary with seeing

[1] Alluding to this, M. Delaborde says, "Is it not noticeable that of all Raffaele's *chefs-d'œuvre* in the Vatican the one which he specially mentions is precisely the least complicated both as to subject and execution, the one perhaps which contains most markedly that reality in type, that unction and simplicity of expression which was eventually to stamp the French painter's own works? It would seem as if Flandrin's earnest admiration for the Mass of Bolsena might be partly because he saw his own presentiments developed therein, and felt at home before that picture which so essentially embodies inspiration without effort, and truthfulness without display."

too much at once, and I do not want to weary of what is beautiful. But in spite of all these things I am sad, especially in the evenings, because I want you. I am alone, and my thoughts always turn to you. I have a magnificent view from my window, and in the evening, when the sun is down, I look out over this great town, over the Campagna beyond, and my gaze loses itself in the vast horizon of the sea. But my thoughts go farther, much farther—to you, and I see you alone, sad, far from your children; the picture saddens me, and I shed tears, which are some relief, and then I turn to a comforting idea, that of my return, and this gives me courage and energy for work."

"*Feb.* 14.—For some time I have been at work, but not as yet very actively. Several things hinder me. First, I have still a good deal to see; then the room and studio which I occupy at present, though most delightful, are only temporary, which keeps me in suspense, and prevents my settling thoroughly. I shall not have my permanent quarters till April. However, I am not losing my time. I am working from Raffaele,[1] and, above all, I profit by the contents of a splendid library. Sometimes I go in the evening to the Director's, where there is often a great crowd,

1. Flandrin made some very interesting studies from the Stanze at this time, which are now in the possession of his pupil, Louis Lamothe.

but that does not suit me best. I like it better when there are not so many people, and when my late travelling companion Thomas plays exquisitely. . . . Yesterday, Boïeldieu, one of the first French composers, who is passing through Rome, came to M. Vernet's salon. Thomas was introduced to him, and then he asked for me, shook hands, and seemed much interested. He has a fine head, which indicates the genius he has displayed."

"*Feb.* 15.—I have just finished some drawings from the antique, for which the Minister sent to M. Vernet, on behalf of a work going on in Paris. The Director applied to me, and I undertook them. Now I am doing some bits from Raffaele, in the Vatican, as a study. Then, as I told you, I read a great deal; and I am learning Italian, at which I am working steadily, because it is so useful, that one can hardly get on without it. We have a great deal to do with Italians, and it is, moreover, a great enjoyment to read and know the great classics of this language; so I work hard at it. To-day I have been taking the portrait of a sculptor student who has finished his time and is returning to Paris—Jaley[1] by name; this

[1] Now member of the Académie des Beaux Arts, and the sculptor of two of the finest modern historical statues in France, Mirabeau and Bailly, executed for the Chambre des Deputés by the order of M. Thiers when he was Ministre de l'Interieur.

will remain in the Academy. . . . . I am on very pleasant terms with all my fellow-students, and have nothing whatever to complain of as concerns them. I hope they may say as much of me. I am very happy here, but I don't want to go to sleep in my *bien-être.* I know what is due to M. Ingres, and his letter, which I read over often, is a constant stimulus to me. May the result justify my efforts!"

There was one drawback to Hippolyte's full happiness, to which allusion is often made. It was the first time in their lives that he and his brother Paul had been separated; and, while thoroughly appreciating the relief from grinding want, and the opportunity of "talking face to face with Raffaele and Phidias," he sorely missed the dear companion who had hitherto shared the hardships of his life, and whom he now craved after to share its pleasures. Writing to Paul, he says: "Rome is sublime in her beauty, but one's mind is not always equally able to enjoy it. I am often very sad, especially in the evening, when I look at the magnificent sunset sky, and my thoughts wander afar. When the lights in the town begin to glimmer I shut my window, and read Plutarch till about nine o'clock, and then I go to bed and read over your letter and M. Ingres', and fall asleep thinking of you and him. . . . . Can it be really true that I have left the Rue Mazarin and the studio, Pont Royal and the city, with her two crowning towers of Notre Dame! I dwell more on all their beauties now that I am absent. This country is delightful, but it will be much more so when we enjoy it together. *Allons*, courage, let us work away! The progress we both make will add to the delight of meeting again!"

Flandrin's letters to his brothers, who were now together in Paris, are full of enthusiastic love for art, and earnest cravings for advance in it both for himself and them.

"ROME, *Feb.* 25, 1833.

"I rejoice to see that you are working hard; I have always felt that Auguste would not have cause to repent of his resolution, and what you Paul and Bodinier tell me of his progress is precisely what pleases me best, because I have confidence in your judgment, and I know that you love him too much to flatter him. Dear Auguste, persevere bravely, and we will all three go on together and help one another. For my own part, I feel greatly the want of an aid and helper; of some one to raise my courage when it fails, as too often happens, and which has already happened here, although amid so much that is new and exciting I ought to be free from such a malady. But it is just because the sight of all these beautiful things makes me long to work, and several misadventures hinder me from working as I should like. First of all, there is no room in the Vatican, it is full of copyists, and if you want to paint you must engage a scaffold three months beforehand. Then, on the other hand, I cannot work at the Academy, because I have not yet got my studio, the man whom I succeed not having finished his last picture. M. Vernet has been so kind as to lend me his studio, but it is so full of his pictures and concerns, and, in honest truth, those are so entirely different from what I want to do, that I cannot stay there long, still less work there. (Don't repeat this to any one; it is not well to get wrong with the people one lives with, especially when there is nothing whatever of which to complain.) But I hope soon to be in my own quarters, for which I shall have waited three months, not in idleness certainly, but to my great inconvenience."

"*March* 1, 1833.—Don't be anxious about my health; I am quite well now. It was only that a little while back, while working in the Vatican, I got a chill, which brought back my pains; but now I have got a good cloak of thick Roman cloth, which is an invaluable defence against the cold, and since that I have worked on without any return of the pains. (However, I beg the aforesaid pain not to look upon this as said in defiance.)

"I was very sorry to hear of M. Ingres' illness, both

because of his own suffering, and because it must delay his picture. I do so dread that it will not be in the Exhibition! and if it appeared now it would be so *à propos!* Everybody's eyes are fixed in expectation on our master, and I really believe that great work would be appreciated. That would be the final stroke of victory, at least I think and hope so with all my heart. . . . You were right to reassure M. Ingres about —— and ——; we seldom meet, and they are working hard. Tell M. Ingres that the only people with whom I talk art are himself, Raffaele and Phidias. I have never had any discussion in the Academy, and hope not to have. Words are not very effectual to convince in such a case; example goes a great deal further; let us try to argue by that means.

"My dear Paul, you talk about music, and Beethoven's Pastoral Symphony. Oh, how I should like to have heard it with you! The way you speak shows that you appreciated it thoroughly. I am fortunate enough to know it, not indeed as executed by the perfect orchestra of the Conservatoire, but admirably rendered on the piano by my good friend Thomas, who gives us some of the best music almost every evening. We have Beethoven, Mozart, and all the best masters in turn, and often there is music in

[1] The Martyrdom of Saint Symphorien. It was not exhibited till 1834.

M. Vernet's salon, when I promise you I am never absent! All the best society comes there. Yesterday evening we had a Grand Duchess of Baden, a Bavarian Princess, and another from Sweden, besides ambassadors, dukes, counts, and countesses, barons and so forth; among whom I often see very fine heads and good draperies. Among the beauties Mademoiselle Vernet is always conspicuous. As to me I look and listen from my corner, and sometimes I actually pluck up courage to cross the salon before everybody!"

"ROME, *March* 25, 1833.

"I was delighted to hear of the sensation caused by M. Ingres' portrait, though I fully expected it. And I was still more pleased to hear that several of his pupils had distinguished themselves, and so bore witness to his sound teaching, and the truth of his principles. . . . Tell M. Ingres that I often take his favourite walk from the Academy to the Coliseum by Santa Maria Maggiore, and always with a little sketch-book in my pocket. I go into the churches and make *croquis.* If you only knew the effect of going into Santa Maria Maggiore! First one is struck by the mysterious gloom which enfolds the choir and aisles, and the perfect stillness which prevails, two or three people only kneeling in a corner. A few days ago I went there, and was startled by this religious impression. All of a sudden a beautiful chant rose from some distant chapel, in the most perfect harmony with all the surroundings. My eye grew accustomed to the darkness, and then I could distinguish the figures in Greek mosaic which decorate the back of the choir, and which are really awful in their greatness. Indeed these old basilicas impress me quite differently from St. Peter's, which is a marvel of grandeur and richness; but duly to estimate it you must use your feet rather than your eyes, for, as one has often heard, it looks far less spacious than it really is."

"ROME, *April* 20, 1833.

"At last I am finally settled in my own room and studio, a nice one of twenty feet square joining my room. It is adorned with some good bas-reliefs, some other casts, all I have in the way of engravings and sketches, and two or three heads I have drawn from Raffaele." [Flandrin also inscribed on one of the panels of his studio the words of Psalm xcii. 4, "Thou, Lord, hast made me glad through Thy works, and I will rejoice in giving praise for the operation of Thy Hands."] "I have left the beautiful view I had over the town for a quieter scene; my present room looks on to the gardens. Between and above the laurel trees I see the fine pines of the Villa Borghese, glimpses of the plain, and towering above all the beautiful snow-covered Sabine hills. It is a wonderfully calm refreshing view. At this moment as I write the sky is bright with stars; I hear no sound save that of a fountain, the plaintive monotonous cry of a bird, and now and then a distant clock striking. There is nothing to remind one of the town. All is calm, silent, beautiful; one can think and dream as one will. Oh! this stillness has a great charm for me, and when I feel it I travel the more readily to you—I see and speak with you! But one must come back to realities, and we shall not meet again this long while yet. Never mind, courage! The thing is to make good use of the time, and that is what I am trying to do. I am making special studies from models in order to overcome the faults I am conscious of. . . . I hear that the Duke of Orléans[1] has ordered a picture of M. Ingres. I am delighted, because at least that will be seen, and nothing more is needed for M. Ingres' paintings."

*To M. Lacuria.*

"ROME, *April* 23, 1833.

" . . . How often I have wanted you to enjoy things with me, for at Paris we shared interests so

[1] This picture was the Antiochus and Stratonice, which was bought by M. Demidoff at the sale of the Duke of Orléans' gallery in 1853, and is now the property of the Duc d'Aumale.

fully! And so amid the Alps, at Milan in the cathedral, at Florence with Masaccio, Giotto and da Fiesole, at Rome with Raffaele and Michael Angelo; in town or country, wherever I am among beautiful things, I think of my brothers, and always including you. I suppose they have shown you my letters, and that you know all about me—so let me tell you what I saw on Easter Day. Early in the morning I went to Saint Peter's. The great piazza was already full of neighbouring peasants, with their wives and children, and among them a great many pilgrims, some coming from far. The greater part were sitting on the ground, waiting for the benediction, which was to be given at noonday. There were wonderfully beautiful groups. Soon the church also filled. The crowd in these churches is not a quiet one as it is in France; there are no chairs, and the people are continually moving and heaving like the waves of the sea. I was fortunate enough to get a good place, and to assist at the Pope's high mass. The ceremonial is magnificent. After mass the Pope went solemnly through the church, carried on a throne by sixteen men, and preceded by all the Bishops now in Rome. I never saw such fine heads as some of the Greek or Armenian Bishops. Then came all the Cardinals, and lastly the Pope. He was carried to a tribune in the midst of the façade of Saint Peter, which commands the piazza from a height of at least one hundred and fifty feet. Everything combined to make this spectacle sublime. The sun, which had been clouded, shone forth at that moment as the Pope appeared in the tribune, sitting on his throne, still raised on his bearers' shoulders. Then the most absolute silence prevailed amid the vast crowd; the Pope rose, spread out his hands, and gave his blessing 'to the city and the universe.' At the same moment the guns fired, their thunder mingling with the sound of bells, drums, bands. I never saw anything so majestic or so solemn. Long shall I remember it!"

"*May* 4.—I often go into the churches. Perhaps I go too much as a looker on, but I cannot help thinking of France, and comparing what one sees there with what goes on here. The churches in Rome are very numerous, and no doubt that is one reason why one finds so few people in them at any given time. I recall the crowds one finds in the Lyons and even in the Paris churches,—how striking and quiet and reverent they are! Here people come and go, talk out aloud, salute their friends and acquaintance, and—specially if it be a high festival—one would hardly believe oneself to be in a church! We complain of the exterior of the Parisian clergy, it is far worse here! But the monks are admirable; they are grave, recollected, and many of them look most entirely religious. I take to them because they have an open, frank manner, which one does not find among the *bourgeois*, and in the matter of physical beauty they are infinitely superior, especially the mendicant orders. I fancy this is because the monks are peasants, or *hommes du peuple*, and these have preserved a very remarkable and characteristic physiognomy, whereas the middle classes and rich people are of the most ordinary type."

"*May* 25.—A few days ago Vibert and I went to see Overbeck, who was good enough to show us his works. We were charmed with the religious spirit which pervades them; and we were specially struck by an immense composition representing the revival of art and science under the influence of religion. It is most beautiful and well conceived, but Overbeck uses means of expression which are not his own; he altogether takes the old masters' garb—he observes nature, but by his own confession he hardly ever has it actually before his eyes when working. Moreover, he aims less at painting than at expressing his thoughts as though in writing. To my mind he is wrong, for if he intends to make use of painting as a way of writing his thoughts, the more true and correct his medium the better the rendering will be. But we came away most pleasantly impressed, talking of the religious impression which Overbeck knows how to give his works, and which always conveys a calm cheerfulness." . . . .

*To his Brothers.*

"ROME, *May* 22, 1833.

"I have just been making a two days' expedition in the neighbourhood. If you could but have been with us! There were my friend Vibert, Stürler, M. Ingres' pupil, Thomas, and three others. I never in all my life saw anything to compare to that beauty. We first crossed a part of the Campagna, which was new to me, intersected by long lines of aqueducts: buffaloes and oxen grazing in the marshes. At Albano we left the carriage, and walked by a delicious path beneath the finest, most beautiful trees I ever saw, the sea, lit up with sunshine, sparkling amid their branches. As far as Ariccia, which is much higher than Albano, it was but one exclamation at the beauty! As for me I could only be silent and gaze on the beautiful sea, which we overlooked from on high, the islands more than twenty miles off, and the Campagna with Rome in the midst, looking merely like a cloud of dust. Directly after we came upon the Lake of Albano, the bed of which is the vast crater of a volcano, on the edge of which stands Castel Gondolfo. The next day we started early on donkey-back. My ass was bigger than ordinary, and just like those which Raffaele has painted in the Loggia. We went slowly through fine woods to the top of Monte Cavo, whence there is the most marvellous panorama imaginable. After revelling in it a long while, we came down again, passed through the village Rocca di Papa, and went to Grotta Ferrata, where we visited Domenichino's fine frescoes. Thence to Frascati, and at last back to Rome, eager for work, as the people in all those places struck me quite as much as the scenery. The women are most exquisitely beautiful—such grandeur, such breadth! Here indeed are Raffaele's models! He took them from this beautiful nature—nature who, queenly and supreme as she is, gives so freely to those who woo her with humble cravings."

"ROME, *July* 17, 1833.

"My dear Paul,—I am very sad after seeing our dear comrade Deroches[1] drowned before my eyes without the possibility of saving him. Some twenty of us had gone to bathe, only about ten being able to swim, of whom Deroches was one. They all went up about a mile higher than we who could not swim, meaning to come down the stream. Only Deroches stayed behind, and, in spite of all we could say, he would

[1] Deroches was a young painter (not an Academy student) working at Rome. His mother had just joined him, and the next day he was to start for France with her. He had stopped in the midst of packing for this bathing party.

cross the Tiber; but, coming back, he got exhausted in the most rapid part of the current. I saw him raise his hands for help, I heard his last cry of agony. It was horrible! I shall never forget it! He never reappeared, and there was nothing to be done. You can imagine our despair. A moment after the others came down. Perhaps if they had been there Deroches might have been saved! Then his poor mother had to be told. The next day we returned to the spot, in hopes of recovering the body, and rendering it the last offices, but all efforts were in vain. Three days later I went with two other men to verify the body, which had been brought to shore. It was him, but terribly disfigured. We buried him in a church near the Academy—his poor mother was gone. I cannot tell you how all these sad events have told upon me, it seems all like a horrible dream. That poor young fellow, so full of hopes—all come to an end. And now M. Guerin[1] is dead. He died yesterday, after more than two months' failure. Madame Horace never left him, and Bodinier did all that a son could do for him. He is a real friend! To-day is the burial, to-morrow a service. You see what a sad chain of events it is."

It was only a year before Flandrin's earnest desire was fulfilled, and his brother Paul rejoined him

[1] Horace Vernet's predecessor as Director of the Academy.

at Rome. Hippolyte, as usual, was thoroughly unselfish, sharing all his small means with his brother, and even contriving, though not without the greatest difficulty and constant self-denial, to send his mother, from time to time, sums which, however small they may seem as compared with the lavish expenditure of wealthy people, were large and important both to giver and receiver in this case.

In March 1833, Flandrin writes to his brother Paul:—"Tell me in your next letter if you sent mama what I told you, and what you have taken yourself from my money in M. Ingres' hands. I only want to know what we actually have, for remember that when you need it my money is yours and theirs as much as mine." And again:—

"*Oct.* 20, 1833.— . . . I send this letter under cover to our cousins, because I have things to say which will not do for a family letter. . . . I want to know what you have done about the money we had in Paris. . . . Tell me, and also about any other little resources you may have. If only I had my 3000 francs at my own disposal, then we should both be well off, whereas now I am in a close fit myself. For the last ten months I have been trying to lay by 100 francs for mama, but I have not managed it. Yet you know that I am not a spendthrift! nor have I become one. But I will explain to you how, with 3000 francs a year, one may be without a sou to spare. You see 2100 francs are deducted for board and lodging, and medical advice if needed. So then there remain 900 francs, to pay for attendance, tailor, shoemaker and laundress, light, wood (and already I am obliged to have a fire for my model), canvas, models, and all other appliances. So you see there is a superabundance in one direction and positive stint in the other. One is very comfortable at the Academy, one wants for nothing, but nevertheless one has not means to get as many models as one requires. All the fellows who do anything of consequence for their *envois*[1] spend five or six hundred francs more than their pension, and that is what I am unable to do.—But to return to your matters, we shall find you some resources here. . . . You may do these things from time to time, without really neglecting your other studies. Oh, when you see these landscapes! How often I have delighted to think of the pictures you may make from them! You will find Poussin and his grand simplicity at every turn. There is no landscape painter here who has got eyes in his head, but when you see the Roman Campagna you will paint it as it is.

[1] The "envois" were pictures which, according to the original rules of the French Academy, her students at Rome were bound to send to Paris from time to time as guarantees that they were really studying and advancing in their profession.

You will advise me, I shall advise you, and we shall renew the old student life I love so dearly. . . ."

Early in January 1834, Paul Flandrin arrived at Rome, and then Hippolyte was able to go on working at his "envoi," which for very excitement in the delightful prospect had come to a standstill, and was reposing with its face to the wall, until the young artist should feel steady enough to continue it. In the September of 1833 Flandrin had sent his brother Paul a sketch of this proposed picture, in order that it might be submitted to M. Ingres. It was done from nature, and the sketch selected was chosen out of sundry attempts.

"The subject is from the Iliad. At the moment when the Grecian army gathered to make a fresh assault on the town, Polites, Priam's youngest son, trusting to his agility, ventured alone among the Trojans to remain without the walls, and seated on the tomb of the ancient Æsetes, he watched the Greeks. I want advice on another matter. Next year I must make my copy (another *envoi*), and after seeing innumerable fine works, I have fixed on Raffaele's glorious Galatea. It is a great undertaking, but still I should like it very much. It has such breadth and vigour, and is at the same time so fair![1]

[1] Flandrin eventually gave up copying the Farnese fresco, and his *copie d'envoi* was from the School of Athens. It is now to be found in the École des Beaux Arts.

If M. Ingres approves, you see what my picture would be. Here, the only idea is to paint great pictures, but I am less ambitious, and though I may be laughed at, I should be quite content if it were possible for me to paint one good figure. I hold that I came to Rome not so much to paint pictures as to acquire the power of painting them."

" ROME, *Dec.* 24, 1833.

" . . . When I began my figure I resolved to show it to nobody, but you can't imagine how difficult that is ! First of all, I was obliged out of respect to show it to M. Horace Vernet. He examined it for a long time, and said, 'I confess honestly that I was not prepared for this, it is very original and in very good tone.' But one can't trust to that. Since I have been forced, will you, nill you, to show it to others who have praised it highly, but as to reckoning upon all that ! ! . . . To you, brother, I look for real frankness,—it is the truest proof of friendship which can be given."

About this time Flandrin's eyes became a source of trouble to him ; the first allusion to this anxiety is in a letter to his brother Auguste dated May 3, 1834, and his usual tenderness for his mother appears in his regret that a letter of a few days' earlier date may have fallen into her hands and alarmed her about his eyes. " I complained a good deal of them, and asked you to consult Cousin Beaumers. It is a great trouble to me! It is a weakness in my good eye, and for the last six weeks I have done nothing in order to give it rest, which is almost the only remedy suggested. But don't make yourself unhappy, for the last few days it has been rather better; only I do regret all the time it makes me lose!"

It was becoming now a question of Ingres succeeding Horace Vernet as Director of the French Academy in Rome, and in the same letter Flandrin alludes to this:—"I also told you not to start for Paris till you knew whether M. Ingres is coming to Rome as Director, in which case I should advise you to come here at once. When you see M. Ingres you will know, here it is spoken of as a thing settled and done. Give him our love, and beg him to forgive me for not having yet made the little sketch he wants from his picture at the Trinità di Monti.[1] I looked out in vain for a moment when I could get the *ensemble.* However, as the time for sending *envois* grew near, I went to try and copy as much as I could see, when my poor eyes put an invincible hindrance in the way. It is very hard that casual circumstances should make us who love our dear master so much seem ungrateful; he asked Paul to copy a head of St. Peter in the Vatican,

1 Our Lord giving the keys to St. Peter,—a picture now in the Luxembourg Gallery.

and Paul has never yet been able to get near it. The hall of the Disputa is full of Russians making enormous copies, and during the year and a half I have been here, though I have been longing to copy some heads, I have never succeeded. But Paul has bespoken a place, and the first thing he means to do is this head for M. Ingres. Tell him all this."

In spite of Flandrin's personal pleasure in the prospect of Ingres coming to Rome, he regretted it professionally. "In my private opinion," he wrote to his brother, "it is a misfortune for art. The thought of seeing him again delights me, but I grieve that he should forsake a position in which he had so desirable an influence over art in France." And in another letter he says:—"In coming here I regret to see him give up the works he was about to execute, and which, being permanently located in Paris, (one was the decoration of a chapel in Saint Sulpice, the other some wall painting in the new church of Notre Dame de Lorette,) in places open to all the world, would have taught so many people, for I believe that in order to correct the judgment of a perverted public you must constantly show them what is really good. M. Ingres has done this already, and it has not been duly appreciated, but it is a question of education. People must have what is really beautiful before their eyes till they get accustomed to it."

To M. Ingres himself Flandrin wrote a little later :—

"Rome, *July* 25, 1834.

"My dear Master,—Now that all uncertainty is over, we may give ourselves up to the pleasure of seeing you again, as is but natural. You have done so much for us, showed such real interest in us! And so you are coming back to beautiful Rome, and I trust it will give you all the rest and quiet you need, and that you will leave the endless worries of Paris behind you. Meanwhile you will work, and your paintings will be constantly teaching the right road in France.

"M. Vernet tells me that he has written to you, and that he by no means congratulates you on coming here. I could not help telling him that I thought it would have been kinder to say so before your appointment than after. If M. Vernet has had some trifling annoyances, it is generally considered due to the *légèreté* of his character, which nevertheless is full of kindness. I, who have never received anything but kindness from him, am of this mind; and I only speak out so freely because I am afraid his letter may have prejudiced you against the students here, who are all full of respect and esteem for you. I am sure that they have only to know you and love you. We ourselves are only too happy in regaining our dear master and his good advice, and we anticipate the day of meeting longingly. . . .—Your grateful and respectful pupil."

Meanwhile Flandrin's *envoi*, Polites, had reached Paris, and he writes to Auguste, September 22, 1834:—"Thanks for what you tell me about my *envoi.* I foresaw M. Ingres' judgment; I knew all its faults, but I did not feel that I could correct them save in another picture. I was setting to work in good earnest when the affection of my eyes came to make me lose this year during which I reckoned on making some progress. I do regret it bitterly. I should have been so glad to show M. Ingres something better. But to have nothing at all! However, as my eyes are pretty well now, I am beginning another picture. If I could express all I feel it would be better unquestionably. Please give my love to M. Ingres, and tell him that I see all the justice of his criticisms on my *envoi*, which are so much good advice which I shall try to use. And please thank him in behalf of us all for the interest he takes in all that concerns us. I think he hardly knows how much we love him. Make my respects to Madame Ingres, and say that if we may know the day of their arrival at Rome, and it will not annoy them, some of us would like very much to go out and meet them."

"ROME, *Oct.* 28, 1834.

" . . . I have been glad to see in the newspapers that my figure has not been thought ill of. Indeed it has been more praised than I expected, and I am glad that M. Ingres has had no annoyance on that score. . . . . I have begun a picture which I should like to have presentable against M. Ingres' arrival. The canvas is ten feet high, the subject taken from Dante's Purgatorio; eleven figures in the foreground. You see I have embarked in a great undertaking, and I fear M. Ingres may not approve of it, but now it is some way on, and I must do my best. If only you had been here you should have been my model for Virgil! Don't mention this picture to any one."[1]

"ROME, *Feb.* 18, 1835.

"My dear Papa,— . . . I am working with all my might for the Exhibition, which opens in six weeks.[2] M. Ingres seems satisfied with my picture, but not so I myself; I should like to begin something else in hopes that it might be better. Paul too works hard, and I expect his progress will be rapid under M.

[1] This picture was exhibited in 1836, and won the second medal. It was bought soon afterward by the town of Lyons for 3,500 francs, and is now in the Museum.

[2] According to the former rules of the French Academy there was an exhibition every spring of the students' *envois*, after which they were sent to France.

Ingres' advice, and that we shall soon see some good landscapes of his. M. Ingres seems very happy here. He has been so well received by all the first artists of every nation; and he found so much order, regularity and harmony among the students, that he was quite touched, and has said so repeatedly."

"ROME, *May* 9, 1835.

"My dear Auguste,— . . . Our exhibition has just closed; I wish you and papa and mama too could have seen it, for M. Ingres expressed keen satisfaction, and I have been congratulated by many artists; but still I am not the more satisfied with myself, and I am very far from going to sleep over it! What really pleased me (this is only between ourselves) was the satisfaction M. Ingres showed on the first day of the Exhibition. While first my figure[1] and then my picture were being hung, his eyes sparkled with delight, and as he passed me, he gave me a private squeeze of the hand, and every time I have seen him since he has spoken in the most hearty and encouraging manner."

"PISA, *June* 15, 1835.

"My dear Papa,—A fortnight ago we set out, Paul, Oudiné and myself. We have already seen Viterbo, Orvieto, Bolsena, Aquapendente, Sienna, Volterra,

[1] A figure of Euripides, now in the Musée at Lyons.

and many smaller places, which are all interesting because of what they contain either in architecture, painting or sculpture; and everywhere we made sketches, which will be valuable remembrances, and which we shall like to show you. It is very pleasant to walk, but horribly tiring in such weather. It is only prudent to walk from three in the morning till nine or ten o'clock, and then again after four or five in the afternoon. Thanks to neglecting this rule two or three times, we are about the colour of mahogany, and my slender beard and moustaches come out quite white against our tint! but we will not make it any deeper, and will be more careful."

*To Eugène Roger.*

"ROME, *Aug.* 1, 1835.

"According to promise I will tell you all we did after parting at the Porta Perugina. Florence was lovely as seen from the hills we ascended, and as usual when leaving anything I became full of regrets. We often looked back, but in about two hours Florence finally disappeared. In the middle of the night we halted at San Giovanni, Masaccio's country. Then slept at Castiglione. The next morning we went under Cortona, but the great heat prevented us from even thinking of going up. Lake of Thrasimene—awful heat; *cicali* such as I never saw or heard before! Once at Perugia we were greatly pleased, and would fain have stayed there more than two days, but Assisi lured us on. We were astounded by our visit to San Francesco. It is not merely the finest collection of pictures of that school I ever saw, but they pleased me more than any others. Cimabue and Giotto are marvellously great! However, we were tired with the last two months' work, and could not do much; and, bothered by the daily storms, we left on the sixth day, promising ourselves to return on purpose, and we still have to see Foligno and Spoleto. During the three last days of our journey, we did not know how to express our admiration for the beautiful scenery through which we were passing; but amid all this we were pestered with one terrible nuisance—the fleas! I never saw anything like it. Only fancy, in the carriage all four of us had to set to work at one fellow's leg to get him something like clear!

"At Otricali we saw Mount Soracte and Monte Cavi again, and I must confess we were very glad to do so. We got back to Rome two months from our start to a day. Adieu! Ton camarade bien affectionné."

"ROME, *Aug.* 15, 1835.

"My dear Auguste,—I understand your reasons, and highly approve of your resolution not to leave our parents while there is any fear of cholera attacking our city. It is an excellent reason, and I would that Paul and I could help you to comfort and encourage our parents. Your other reasons strike me as feeble. Dear fellow, do what you think best, but consider all I told you, and believe always in the sincere love of your brothers. I reckon on that love as the real happiness of my life—*our* life, I mean to say.

"I should have liked you to know our musician, Ambroise Thomas, with whom I have formed a real hearty friendship. He taught me to understand the real beauty of music. Every one loves and esteems him. For nearly three years we have benefited by him as man and as artist, and by his admirable talent; but there is an end to everything! He must go, and I feel it very deeply. Since I have been here I think I am much more sensitive to these things, and yet they have come so often over and over again! Nearly the whole Academy has been changed since I came; I have had time to get attached to my comrades, and then one by one I have seen them go, and Thomas is the last, and quite the greatest loss I can have. Without Paul I should be quite alone. . . . . The lovely music which I heard daily has become a necessity to me. It had become a remedy against the frequent attacks of discouragement which murder one and destroy the best part of one's life. . . . .

*P.S.*—We have just heard of the abominable crime of July 28th,[1] and, like every one that loves his country, we were horrified."

"ROME, *Aug.* 16, 1835.

"My dear Papa,— . . . As the cholera is approaching Rome, to spare you anxiety through exaggeration, I may as well tell you that it is at Leghorn, sixty miles hence. At present there does not seem much to fear, and it may leave us on one side. People say that the situation of Rome, in an entirely volcanic country, is favourable; we shall see. And if it comes, Paul will come to me, we shall go out but little, and spend the evenings with M. Ingres. After all, the best thing is to wait patiently, and have trust in God. You bid us pray to God for you, dear Papa. We never fail to do so, but assuredly we shall do so now with double earnestness, and on our side we look with comfort to your prayers for us."

The close affection between the three brothers is very touching; simple and unassuming as he was, Hippolyte always seems to be forced into the position of eldest, rather than Auguste, who was actually the senior. Probably Hippolyte's position as an Academy prizeman, and his superiority of means, small as that was, were partly the cause of his being involuntarily

[1] Fieschi's attempt.

treated as leader. His little bits of brotherly advice are generally accompanied with some unselfish offer or suggestion. Thus he writes, urging Auguste (who was taking portraits at Lyons) to "work at them as if they were studies. Don't let the thought of money creep into them, for it spoils whatever it touches. All the same, don't let that hinder you from asking a better price than you have hitherto done."

Hippolyte and Paul were always longing to have the trio united, and in the autumn of 1835 their wish seemed likely to be realised. The French Government commissioned Ingres, as Director of the Academy in Rome, to have copies made of all Raffaele's pictures in the Loggia and Stanze of the Vatican, and he wished to associate Auguste Flandrin with his brother Paul in the work. It does not exactly appear why Auguste declined the offer, but Hippolyte writes, Sept. 29, 1835: "Paul is working at his copies from Raffaele's Loggia. I have seldom seen anything so difficult to copy, but he is doing it very well, and between ourselves, we cannot help being very sorry that, after being selected by M. Ingres, you should not be able to come; for this work, while it forces one to make real progress, would have brought you in useful supplies, and would probably have enabled you to try a picture. However, it is not quite a lost chance, for, if you come later, I hope M. Ingres will give you some of the copies to make. Only yesterday he told me how sorry he was not to see you at work there. . . . . Paul works all day at the Vatican, and I in my studio at my *envoi.* It is a figure (called the Jeune Berger); and besides that I have a picture in hand for the magnificent Cathedral of Nantes. The subject is fine—St. Clair restoring sight to the blind. The scene is at Nantes, where St. Clair was Bishop in the third century, and my canvas is nine feet high. The Bodiniers arranged it. They proposed to me to paint the picture, and I accepted with great pleasure, so as to do something that has a destination. As to the price we must say nothing about that. I am doing fifteen figures, the size of life, for a thousand francs, pretty much what the expenses will be—but what would you have? I would rather that than be obliged to hire a lumber-room."

*To M. Ambroise Thomas.*

"ROME, *Jan.* 20, 1836.

" . . . . As you say, you have returned to an active life, I, as well as all who know you, hope that you will neglect nothing, that you will seize opportunities, and that before long we shall hear you spoken of. If such opportunities occur, do not lose your courage. Work, always work on. It will not be lost, even if there were no other result than strengthening your powers. I remember you used to say yourself that to write well a man must write much. . . . . I will tell you what we are all about. Jouffroy has just finished a very beautiful figure. Husson, who has three months' extension of his time, is getting on with his group. Simart is doing a great bas-relief, which promises well; Oudiné a figure, with which M. Ingres is delighted. Jourdy and Brian have each a figure in hand. In architecture I am best acquainted with Baltard's *envoi*, which is very interesting and well done. As to Elwart, he is composing comedies, dramas, songs, and odes; besides cantatas, duets, trios, and ever so many masses. He works as hard as possible. For myself, I have almost finished my figure, and am getting on with my picture, which began with ten figures, and now has seventeen,—a little bit of dear old Thomas, which everybody recognises, is one."

*To the Same.*

"ROME, *March* 17, 1836.

"Yesterday M. Ingres came to me in the salon, and squeezing my hand, said in a whisper, 'Oh, how more than ever I miss him!' He did not mention your name, but we are so much in the habit of talking of you that I quite understood. Your letter and the little bit of Beethoven [an autograph] pleases him much. By this time you will have seen Oudiné, and perhaps Elwart. Instead of them we have got Farochon, and also Boulanger, who seems a very good sort of fellow. I am so glad you gave him your waltzes. I often linger in the corridor to hear him practising them. . . . What of Meyerbeer's new opera? [the Huguenots, just out.] Mind and tell me in your next letter."

*To M. Lacuria.*

"ROME, *March* 24, 1836.

"It is so long since I sent you a friendly word, that, although I have nothing to write with save my left hand or the two middle right fingers, I must not hesitate to begin. The cause of my incapacity is this. After finishing both my picture and figure, with back and chest broken and eyes worn out with tire, I intended to set myself up again by a little expedition to the sea, returning by the mountains; when, choosing some brushes in a shop, and using my nail vigorously to draw them out of a packet, the wood split, and a splinter went up under the nail as far as the first joint. I had to run half over the town to find a surgeon who could take it out, and the result has been a great deal of pain, and instead of a tour I have been condemned to keep my room and be starved! But don't be alarmed—I am much better.

"Janmot has a letter from you, in which you abuse

yourself tremendously for having—so you say—written all manner of nonsense to me about my picture. I don't agree with you. I thought some of your advice very useful, and I have kept it. My studio is in such a mess that I can't just now put my hand on your letter, so I cannot refer to it, but I will answer from memory. First of all; as I like your tone, I was very pleased to read your praise of certain parts which myself, too, I think the best. Then, looking at it as a whole, you say that you do not recognise Hell, or the expression of fear which is so prevailing in Dante. But here you are mistaken; it is Purgatory that is treated, and the predominant feeling in Dante's mind is not fear, but pity: a feeling which I have tried to express by Dante's action, that of consoling the suffering souls. As to the criticism that there is a lack of power in the expression, I entirely agree with it. Dante's poetry is quite another thing. It has often made me afraid with a sublime fear; but to convey that one needs something far beyond the talent of a man who can see, or fancies that he sees, what is true beauty at intervals as transient as lightning, and then grows lost in the analysis of form, tone, and all that is purely mechanical. It is the trouble which the mechanical part is to me which involves so poor a result in expression. I feel and confess it, and yet (perhaps I may be mistaken) it does not seem to me a reason for avoiding difficult subjects, and that because one never shakes off pettiness of handling so well as when subject to a predominant thought. I think that ought to enable one to improve far more than aimless studies. To my mind, the more one asks the more one gets. Ask a great deal, and you will get a little; ask but little, and you get—nothing! I am not sure if you will understand me, anyhow I am sure that you would understand what I want to say if I were talking. It is so difficult to write these things!

"I have finished my other picture, my Saint Clair, and M. Ingres came to see it. If you only knew how encouraging he was! Well, I think I must tell you all about it, on condition that it goes no further. He came in, sat down in front of the picture, and for a bit said nothing. I was confused, and so was Paul. At last he got up, looked at me, and embraced me warmly—you know his way—saying, 'Well, *mon ami*, art is not lost, and I have not been useless!' I felt very small to be the subject of such words, and did not know how to speak, only my tears fell. The dear good man was so happy! I shall never forget that minute! But I could only tell such a thing to a friend like yourself, my dear Lacuria; you must see as well as I do that it would damage me in the sight of others.

"I remember your asking me some time ago if I really loved this country? Somehow I cannot express what I feel. I love France dearly—my parents and friends are there, and assuredly I love it best; but when I think of leaving Rome I am heart-broken. When I look from my window on that beautiful plain, and the fine chain of Sabine mountains—those fine mountains with their grand old names; and then at our lovely garden, and at the old palace where I dwell; when I see all this from one window, and then turning to the other I command the whole town, with the sea line in the horizon, I cannot bear to think of leaving it all. It will cost me a great deal, but it must be done; I feel that I ought not to live here. . . ."

*To M. Ambroise Thomas.*

"ROME, *April* 30, 1836.

" . . . Yesterday I was alone; it was very fine, and I went to the upper galleries of the Coliseum, where I had never been since you left. How childish one is! Coming to that last arch, I was quite overcome. However, I got there, and nothing is changed, except that the two little seats, intact, are surrounded with big plants and flowers. I thought of you, and recalled what you said one day as we were going up the Pincio, about our being happy if some day we could make a name, and attain some reputation as artists. I re-echoed you; and now we must remind one another of it, for such a stimulus is helpful. There are still two years before we shall meet again,—two of our best years: they should be well spent."

Amid all this enthusiastic devotion to his art and artist friends, the parents at Lyons were never forgotten; the same warm outpourings of love which went to them from the young boy first leaving home continued to cheer M. and Mme. Flandrin in regular succession from Rome, and one of the first thoughts, amid any credit won or prizes obtained, was sure to be the pleasure it would give at home. Thus he writes to his parents (June 1, 1836): ". . . I often look at a little sketch I made long ago, of Lyons from the heights of Montesuy. I think of you there, waiting for us, and then the time seems very long! But, on the other hand, when I think of the work done, it seems so little, and time to have gone so quickly by! However, I can conscientiously say that I have worked hard, and I feel that I have advanced."

And to Ambroise Thomas (June 14) he says: "I hear from you and from Bodinier that I have got a medal. I am very glad for my father's sake. Bodinier will give it to him *en passant*."

This was a second class gold medal for the picture from Dante, and the following year the Saint Clair won a first gold medal. Flandrin was then preparing for his last *envoi*,—a picture now at Lisieux. He was very reserved about it, and made all his fellow-students promise not to look at it until it was finished, wishing to be uninfluenced by any comments or criticism save those of his brother Paul. So far did he carry this fancy, that wanting very much to use a student, Dominique Papety by name, as a model—Papety having remarkably well-formed hands—Flandrin almost gave him up rather than reveal his secret! The good-natured fellow met his friend's difficulty by offering to come and sit blindfold! and in this way the resolution was kept. Flandrin writes to his friend, Ambroise Thomas:—

"ROME, *June* 14, 1836.

"I have fixed upon a Scriptural subject I have always loved, and which M. Ingres approves highly. I take the moment when the Jewish women brought their children to Jesus Christ that He might bless them, the disciples repulsing them, and Jesus rebuking the disciples, saying, 'Suffer the little children to come unto Me, and forbid them not, for of such is the Kingdom of Heaven.' I can imagine a wonderfully beautiful scene; the grand meaning and feeling stamping our Lord's words afford a magnificent opening, but it is an alarming thing to undertake. M. Ingres' approbation encourages me greatly. I was afraid he might have preferred something else, but, on the contrary, he was delighted with this subject. All this is between ourselves, please. Until my picture has got on, I shall say nothing about it to any one. Besides, I shall hardly begin to paint it before January, having my sketch to make, a copy, and a journey to Naples."

"ROME, *July* 8, 1836.

"My dear Auguste,—Flacheron tells me that there is to be an Exhibition of Paintings at Lyons in October, and as I often grieve that papa never sees anything we are doing, I have a mind to send my Dante. Flacheron also says something which encourages me to do this, namely, that the town will have from forty to fifty thousand francs to spend, and, who knows? they might perhaps buy my picture! M. Ingres is vexed that it was not bought at Paris, but there is no good thinking about that now—it is over. So will you find out about the exhibition, and when pictures should be sent in, and then write to Lacuria, or any one else who cares enough for us to take the trouble, and ask him to go to the École des Beaux Arts, and reclaim the Dante and the Shepherd, and have them packed with the frames they had in the Louvre. It must all be done as cheaply as possible, for they have already cost me about eight hundred francs, and I am hardly disposed to sell the clothes off my back for so uncertain a chance.

"I am so glad to tell you that the other day, while

Paul was working at the Vatican, a fellow-student helped me to sell two of his landscapes. That gives him a little nest-egg of eight hundred francs, which came at a good time, for that very morning he found he only possessed a baiocco and a half, or about two sous! I am particularly glad, because I was afraid he would not have been able to come to Naples with me, and I could not have helped him. Working as I do, I am not rich enough to lend fifteen francs to anybody!—not a very brilliant position, as you perceive, but so happy in many ways, that I think I shall always look back to this time longingly!"

The Dante was exhibited at Lyons, and was bought, as Flandrin hoped, by the municipality for 3500 francs. His figure of Euripides was also bought by the town for 1000 francs. The Shepherd, which was sent to Lyons with Dante, was going to be purchased by Flandrin's old Lyonnese master, Legendre-Héral, but, with his usual kindliness and liberality, Flandrin refused to accept a price, and gave it to the Professor, who in return volunteered to execute a bust of his father for Hippolyte. This was joyfully accepted. He bids Auguste tell Héral "how grateful we are, and how pleased at the prospect. I cannot say how delighted I am to have a portrait of our father, and by him! Tell him that I think my Shepherd has found a better position than I looked for, and that his approval is a weighty encouragement to me. He must excuse my writing myself, my head is very weak, and I cannot get rid of fever. We have lately been at Albano, to try change of air as a last remedy. The first few days we were both better, but the fever returned, and now we are back at Rome, waiting to see what time will do. However, Paul is something better, and perhaps he will shake it off before the spring. Don't say anything about it to papa and mama; but I must confess to you that it is very unfortunate for us to be losing such precious time!"

It was a terrible time of fever, and all the strangers residing in Rome seem to have suffered. Flandrin writes to Ambroise Thomas:—

"ROME, *Aug.* 29, 1836.

". . . . This is one of the worst years for fever. In the Villa Medici alone, M. and Mme. Ingres, Simart, Jourdy, and Boulanger (twice over) have had it, and I am just getting better. I was comfortimg myself by preparing for our journey to Naples, where we were to meet Baltard, and my eldest brother was to join us. Our plans were magnificent! But it all had to be given up. Cholera has broken out severely at Ancona; all communication with the kingdom of

Naples is suspended, no passports given; and I have written to my brother to defer his journey, for if the cholera should come here, it would be stupid for him to come so far to meet it! So farewell to lovely Naples, which I accept on the faith of your descriptions. Without having ever seen it, I seem to know it, and even to have most lively recollections thereof! I should have looked for well-known footsteps, and names inscribed. I feel quite familiar with the Hermit of Vesuvius' book! Doesn't all this make you think that one forgets less quickly at Rome than in Paris? It may be so, eh? and does not seem unlikely. Ah, well, *mon ami*, all this charming prospect of journey, excursions and expeditions has been exchanged for fever and the alarm of cholera!

"My life is perhaps still more recluse than when you were here, and that is a year and nine days ago, which upon calculation shows me that I have still more than sixteen months. Poor dear Rome, how shall I leave her? The other night, before going to bed, I took a chair and sat out on the balcony to enjoy the moonlight view of the town. It was one of those nights when the light, coming from behind the masses of buildings, throws them out so well. The frogs croaking and the fountain splashing did not mar the silence which prevailed, their monotony almost seemed to blend with and increase it. There was not a motion, not a light. Just as I was going in a few chords of a piano fell upon my ear—and oh! they brought back so much that . . . . *Basta!* I was only going to tell you that I should be very sorry to leave Rome, although it will be to see my parents and friends."

The alarm of cholera was serious. Hippolyte wrote a little later to Auguste:—"Cholera is making great destruction at Ancona, but as yet it has not advanced further. The French garrison has behaved very grandly. Finding that the terrified natives forsook the sick, General Cubières asked for volunteers to go and nurse the cholera patients, and almost all the soldiers came forward, and rivalled one another in zeal. Supplies were wanting, for the neighbourhood sent in nothing; but the French General set that straight by threatening to make a sally with the garrison and pick up whatever he could lay hands on for the town."

The malady spread to Naples in spite of precautions, and Flandrin had reason to rejoice that he had not gone there. He writes to his old friend Eugène Roger (October 31, 1836):—" . . . . Baltard has not returned, for the cholera broke out at Naples before he left it, and he is obliged to make a sort of quarantine for three weeks at Sora, with his wife and child. It was partly his own fault, for it was not hard to foresee how it would be. At Naples there are already as many as two hundred and fifty cholera cases daily. It seems as if it must come here before long, and yet who knows? It has spared Lyons. You have heard how grandly our fine soldiers have behaved at Ancona; the Italians let them have an easy monopoly of courage and self-devotion. I must tell you a story. Just lately one of our last year's students, Famin, an architect, was making an expedition to Anagni without a passport, when the Governor of the town arrested him, and sent him from one prison to another in chains. As soon as he got free and reached Rome, he went straight off to M. de Latour-Maubourg. It was nine in the morning. The Ambassador wrote off a thundering letter to the Cardinal Secretary of State, who appeared himself by noon to make excuses for the Government, and to say that a courier was already despatched to recall the Governor of Anagni, and order him to Saint Angelo, where he has now been a week. The Ambassador further insisted on a circular describing the assault and its punishment being sent to all the Governors of towns in the Roman State. We are well pleased with our Ambassador, and very grateful to him for avenging us of such treatment so speedily.

"What you tell me of X. is very grievous. . . . . Accumulating work, undertaking everything, and receiving money, is not all that a man has to think of! I agree with you, that in such matters one's character as a man must be borne in mind as well as one's talents as an artist.

"We have had a terrible autumn. Rome has been devastated with fever, and at the Academy almost everybody, from the Director to the porter, has had their turn. I am just getting over my third attack, and I very much fear that it will not let me get my copy quietly done."

"ROME, *Feb.* 12, 1837.

"My dear good Mama,— . . . . I am quite sure you shared my pleasure when the town bought my pictures. It is a piece of good fortune which I want to share with you. I know, dear little mother, how much you dislike living in a dirty apartment, and if nothing has been done to ours since I left, I am sure by this time it must be very little to your taste. So will you please, dearest mama, to do me a pleasure, and accept the little sum of one hundred francs for some improvements, if they can be done without putting papa out? In that case you must take the money for anything else you will. Auguste will be my banker and give it you. You will take it, dear little mother, won't you, and try to beautify your small abode? Auguste was to have come here in January, but I begin now to despair of seeing him before I go. Yet he might have got so much good from it. I hope at least he will remember how persistently I have begged and entreated him to come. Adieu, dearest mother. I pray daily for you and for our dear father. I am quite sure that neither do you forget us, and I attribute all the good things which befall me to my darling mother's prayers."

*To M. Ambroise Thomas.*

"ROME, *Feb.* 13, 1837.

" . . . . After a dreary rainy winter, spring begins to cheer us now. The bright sun and flowering trees recall one of our first walks—we bought fir cones and oranges at the Quattre Fontane, and went to eat them at Caracalla's Baths. . . . . Here, as the cholera is dreaded, the Carnival was forbidden; but as the Romans bore the privation patiently, though regretfully, they were permitted to have the Moccoletti on the last day. The Corso was full, and everything seemed all right, but the first moccoletti were hissed and forcibly extinguished: there was quite a hubbub with carriages getting out of the row, shops shutting, and all the rest of it; and now it is called 'the Revolution of the Moccoletti,' and, as usual, the Romans say that its chief promoters were the students of the French Academy.

"Your Carnival cannot have been very gay either, with your influenza. We have been very unfortunate here—poor M. Ingres has been very ill. . . . . Paul has not had any fever for two months, so I hope he has done with it; but as for me, I don't seem to have had my share, for it keeps coming back twice in each week. I am waiting impatiently for the amendment which the doctors say spring will make. It has thrown me back so much, that I can assure you I shall have no difficulty in finding occupation from now till April 1838.

"*Feb.* 23.—My letter was delayed by an attack of fever, but to-day I am better. . . . . You ask if I often go over the scenes of our favourite walks? Alas, for a long time I have scarcely stirred! I have only been once to Torre de Schiavi since you left, the violets at Villa Pamfili were gathered without us, and since the day we went together to the Villa Mellini I have never been able to return. *Tre anni, bagatella!*"

"ROME, *June* 18, 1837.

"My dear Auguste,— . . . . You say that we shall soon see you, and that I am not to set off without you; but, my dear fellow, I am not my own master, especially in my present state of health. I am still beset with fever, and the doctors say the month of September must not find me in Rome, or that I shall assuredly be ill all next year again. So I must try to get away in the beginning of August. You can imagine that it is grievous after having worked, and my works having had so much more success than I expected, to be hindered just when a much more important work is in hand, and when I want to collect all my strength, and make a sort of final effort. I feel that I am almost losing even the wish to succeed. Illness and weakness have given me a sort of disgust and depression which follow me everywhere. Shall I really be obliged to give up all my hopes? But, after all, I am not always in this disheartened state. A few days without fever restores some energy, and I feel my love of work again. I have made a beginning of my great picture in one of these intervals, but one ought to be very strong to carry a thing like that through."

"FLORENCE, *Aug*. 24, 1837.

"My dear Auguste,— . . . . In the last days of July, after the terrible news from Sicily, a few cases of cholera appeared in Rome, where the alarm was very great, because Government and the doctors have done everything they could to persuade people that it is contagious. I had been for two months without fever, and was working at my last picture, unfortunately harder than I had strength for. I was to start in August, so as to avoid the fever season, but fatigue brought it on too soon; and just as the first cases of cholera appeared I fell ill again, and the remedies caused violent inflammation. After some days of uncertainty as to whether the plague was among us or not, we were reassured, and M. Ingres and our friends advised us to go away and try to cut my fever short, for fear I might have it through another year. Alas, if I could have foreseen what has happened I would not have gone, and I am sure that I should not have suffered as much in sharing the danger with them as amid the fatigue and anxiety we have experienced. We started, thinking that this attack was only much the same as some thirty or forty attacks I have had since I was at Rome. We took the Sienna route for Florence, August 3rd, in a fearful heat, and with a vetturino, who went like a tortoise, only getting on some ten or twelve *lieues* a-day. And oh! what I suffered, being ill to begin with. When we reached the Tuscan frontier we were met by two men, who informed us that we must go back, as the Tuscan Government had set up a *cordon sanitaire;* and we had to go and lie in quarantine at Aquapendente for a fortnight, a horrid little town. We were five Frenchmen and one German, all artists, and all very good friends. We agreed to go and make out the time at Perugia, a very beautiful place, on a hill, and with a much better air. When we got there they hesitated whether they would let us in or not. It ended by our being admitted, and then I got some fresh fever. However, the quiet suited me, and I was mending. Soon the news from Rome grew alarming, and we heard from a crowd of fugitives that cholera had broken out very decidedly; that there were as many as two, sometimes even three hundred deaths daily, and that our good M. Sigalon was one of the first victims. . . . . How I regretted having left M. Ingres and the Academy under such circumstances! However, as it was impossible to return, and our quarantine was over, we set out for Florence. When we reached the frontier they signalled to us to go back, and some soldiers came out to arrest us. But at last, after a great deal of debating, we were admitted. Two hours later we were dining at Arezzo, thinking ourselves lucky in having at last crossed the Tuscan frontier, when suddenly we heard that the cholera had broken out in Florence. Just think of this. But we had gone too far to turn, so we went on, and on arriving here we found that there have only been one or two cases, which it is hoped will not have any succession. If it should increase we are ready to start, without quite knowing where to go, for cholera is everywhere,—at Rome, Naples, Genoa, Leghorn, Venice. So you see, my dear fellow, we cannot give you any advice as to your journey. . . . . My poor picture! it will indeed be fortunate if it ever gets decently finished. However, we must hope for better times."

*To M. Eugène Roger.*

"SERMIDA, *Oct.* 11, 1837.

"Here we have been for several days watching the Po rush by, and waiting until we can cross it. I must tell you how it has all come about. At Padua we devoured the Titians and Mantegnas, but, above all, the Giottos in Santa Maria del Arena. What a jewel that chapel is! What soft sweet harmony among the Titians! I approve your choice. You will preserve a thing like to perish, and which is most admirable. I imagine you to be at work by this time.[1] After three days we started for Vicenza and Verona. Our first business was to find out whether Verona was healthy, and would do for our quarantine. On first asking we were told that the town was *sanissima*, and a certificate to that effect was given us, but unfortunately we could learn nothing for certain, so we started for Peschiera and the Lago di Garda. And at Mantua they could hardly guarantee the quarantine we proposed keeping; so there was nothing for it but to go to the frontier and make sure. We saw Giulio Romano's frescoes in the Palazzo del Te, and I was surprised, amazed. Certainly in some of them he comes out like an old

[1] Eugène Roger had undertaken to copy a fresco of Titian's in the Scuola di Sant' Antonio at Padua. His copy is now at the École des Beaux Arts.

master. We stayed there three days, not failing to visit the Palazzo del Te daily; and we should have been glad to work there, but the fever traces we saw on so many faces frightened us. I have not had any actual fever since we parted, but I feel that this air is bad for me. I am still weak."

*To M. Ambroise Thomas.*

"ROME, *Dec.* 10, 1837.

"Only twenty days more of my time here! The end is coming, but I shall feel it much more than you. I have still some troublesome things to do. I have to leave this quiet peaceful position, this beautiful country, which—fever notwithstanding—I love more and more—dear M. Ingres and our comrades. Of course I shall have my country and parents and friends instead, and I appreciate the compensation; but still in my heart there is a sad gloomy thought of parting from the soothing stillness one enjoys here, to go and fight in that ant-hill for bread to live upon! If at least I could have waited till I had decided! But no, I feel that I am pushed on, and that I must leave in three weeks. You advise me to go at once and finish my picture in Paris, but indeed I cannot, my dear fellow. I am sure that my picture would suffer, and it has already suffered enough through my bad health and the unfortunate circumstances amid which it has been produced. But I am doing all I can. In fear and trembling at the short time remaining, I am using that to the utmost. . . . My plans are as follows, supposing cholera and other things to agree. I hope to have pretty well finished my picture by the middle of April. Then I shall go to Naples and stay there a month. Thence return to take leave of Rome, and take the steamboat for Marseilles. Then six weeks or two months at Lyons, and by August I hope to embrace you. But you shall hear again. At this moment I hear the *pifferari.* How they recall past times. Yesterday evening we went to the Ponte Molle to meet Roger. It was so pleasant. Alas! alas! I shall never do that again for any one, unless it be for the man who succeeds me!"

The happy meeting with his parents to which Hippolyte Flandrin had looked so continually through his years of study at Rome was not to take place. His father, who had seemingly been in bad health for some time, died just before the expiration of Flandrin's studentship. He writes as follows :—

"ROME, *Jan.* 26, 1838.

"My dearest Mama and poor Auguste,—I will not attempt to dwell on our grief, you know it all by your own. We have lost our good, loving father; and you have both been all you ought to him ; you could prove your love for him, you have fulfilled all your duties —but we ! After an exile of five years, just as we were about to return, our one thought was to see you again, and by our loving care to make up for time lost ; yes, it was really lost, inasmuch as we have not been able to help or comfort you—just at this moment our dear father is gone from us. We could not embrace him or hold his hands, and you have been suffering and weeping without us. It is very hard to bear ! But I am only adding to your grief by all this !

"We thank Auguste warmly for the details he sends us. They are an alleviation you must feel strongly. He is gone, loving us all, upheld by the religious mind we could most have wished for him ;—the holy mind, which can loosen the tenderest bonds without breaking them. What courage that must have given him! I ought to comfort you, and fain would do so ; and it is very trying to us, dearest mama, not to be with you and able to do so as far lies in our power. But I trust to our brother, that dear brother who has done so much for us all, and for whom we feel such boundless gratitude. I trust to your religion, the true source of our courage and all your goodness ; and I trust too to your love for us. Mama, you do wish to live for your three children, don't you? and you will ask God that you may do so, just as we ask it continually?

Oh, if we could but embrace you! I beseech you to be brave and resigned; I rely on it because of your love for us. Do not be anxious about us; we are surrounded by kind friends. . . . Imperative duties detain us here for a while, but we shall lose no time in coming to you. Take care of yourself I beseech you. We pray for our dear father, and for you and for our brother. Do you pray for us too. Adieu, dearest mother, adieu, dear brother and friend."

*To MM. Ambroise Thomas and Harlé.*

"Rome, *March* 16, 1838.

"Dear Friends,—I write hurriedly to you, because, as you guessed, I am working at my picture, and have no time to spare. Your letter was very welcome, and your expressions of friendship all the more precious, that within the last two months we have had a heavy sorrow. We have lost our dear father, and a few days after, one of our comrades, Clerginet, had the same loss. I had finished my time, I was going to see him. . . . O dear friends, it will be a sad return! So you see I have had to work at my unlucky picture amid sickness and sorrow. God knows what it will turn out! Nobody has seen it yet, not even M. Ingres. As for me, I am tired out to the last degree, and am no judge. Adieu, dear old fellows. The sympathy of friends is a true balm, and I know we have yours."

"ROME, *March* 30, 1838.

"Dear Auguste,—I answer your last letter in haste. I was quite sure you would approve our choice. Assuredly our dear mother deserves every proof of confidence and love. Thanks for your good report of her, it is a great comfort to us. Dear fellow, I have had much the same thoughts as you about our weakness. We have no more strength to bear a prolonged sorrow than a very great joy, or a protracted season of rest. Already we sometimes reproach ourselves for beginning to sing again at our work; yet I don't think any one could love a good father more devotedly. His memory is always present, and our regret is very deep. I hope it will soften, and that we shall find comfort in recalling his words and doings to one another's mind."

*To M. Ambroise Thomas.*

"NAPLES, *June* 14, 1838.

"I am writing to you from Santi Combi's on the Santa Lucia, and what is more, from your own old room. Every day I look out on all you love so much,—the beautiful gulf, Vesuvius, the mountains and islands. I have all these, I drink them in and admire them; and yet the beloved Rome is continually rising up before me. I left it on the 4th. Poor M. Ingres! how sorry I am to leave him for two years and a half!

Our comrades were very kind, they went as far as Porta San Giovanni with me; we were twenty-three in all there when we separated. Here we have been already over and over again to the Museum, Pompeii, Herculaneum and Vesuvius, which is very placid at the present moment, but fine all the same. At the Hermitage my first object was to get the book of 1833, and to find your name. I was so pleased to find it I could not resist putting mine by it. I am here; with Paul and my eldest brother, who joined us at last, as also Boulanger and Roger, capital travelling companions. We are starting for Pæstum. Then we propose going by sea to Leghorn, and taking Pisa, Florence and Milan, that our brother may see them. Then a time at Lyons with my dear mother; and early in September we hope to join you, and see what can be done."

*To M. Eugène Roger, Naples.*

"FLORENCE, *July* 6, 1838.

"Here we are, but not without our troubles! For the first seven hours after leaving you our voyage was a sort of enchantment. The sea was superb, mountains and islands put on the most marvellous effects of form and colour, the sun set gloriously behind Cape Circe, the bright moon lit up the sea. All was calm; but towards ten o'clock the wind rose, clouds covered the sky, general *malaise* began to be felt, every one grew restless and began to try to find bearable positions—in vain! On all sides lamentations and grunts! Then came rain, which forced every one to seek shelter, stumbling about and holding on as they could. Inside, such a sight! a downright battlefield. There we stayed, like the rest, stretched pell mell on the floor like so many sacks of corn. The waves were dashing noisily over the deck, and washing down into every corner of the vessel, drenching us all; but I never stirred a finger to avoid getting wet, nor any one else either! However, after three or four hours, by some superhuman efforts, we did contrive to slither into our berths, and there we stayed till ten the next day, when we reached Cività Vecchia. We landed and met Famin and good old Guénepin, who had come to meet us. We wanted to dine with them, but, all in much the same condition, we had to content ourselves with seeing them eat, casting dismal glances the while at the sea dashing up against rocks and ramparts.

"However, we re-embarked bravely, under our friends' auspices, and though the sea was very rough we had not strength left to be as ill as the night before. We stayed huddled up in our holes till we reached Leghorn, where we left Boulanger. The sea was calmer, so I hope he will have got on better. Pisa delighted us, and Florence is always charming to me. In spite of all we have seen at Naples, the old Tuscan masters hold their own to my mind. I delight more than ever in them and in Raffaele."

These last words, written as Flandrin's student life in Italy closed, are noticed by his friend and biographer, Vicomte Delaborde, as a noteworthy *résumé* of the impressions he had received, and a programme of his future work and the earnest aim of his life. "Do we not find the continued proof of this preference for the old Tuscan masters and for Raffaele" (M. Delaborde asks) "more and more in all his works, from the Chapel of Saint Severin to the nave of Saint Germain des Prés? Not that his respectful memories for his great models took shape in mere literal imitation or technical likeness. Hippolyte Flandrin knew too well that, like ancient art, the Italian Renaissance is not a language, the beauty and genius of which can be adopted by the mere outward copyist. Rather than rest content to imitate the exterior of the great works which he took as his permanent models, he devoted himself to studying their spirit, striving to revert to the source whence their inspiration flowed, so that he too might drink thereof. So that while the Stanze of the Vatican are to his mind the most absolute expression of pictorial perfection; while, as he repeatedly would affirm, Giotto's frescoes in Santa Maria del Arena, or those of Fra Angelico in the Chapel of Nicholas V., ought to be 'the very breviary' of the painter of religious subjects, Flandrin none the less sought daily to study on his own account, and to adapt the lessons of the past to the requirements of his personal feeling and the wants of the present day."

Three years spent in Rome had indeed not been wasted. His influence among his fellow-students had been great—it is one of themselves[1] who speaks of it as "a downright fascination to all who came near him —the fascination of a superior artist and a good man;" and the two things were wonderfully blended.

From his birth he had possessed—and they never failed him—the passionate instincts of an artist, a keenness of perception of, and craving for, every expression of external beauty, realising the great truths of all forms of beauty, and irresistibly constrained, so to say, to give it shape; but he was also a Christian, one for whom there could be no beauty save on the condition that it tells of God; one who in the region of the ideal could no more separate his admiration from his belief than he could separate his speculative knowledge from his actions in daily life. The most perilous days of early youth were steered through in safety by the help of a pious childhood, and the wholesome examples of

[1] Ambroise Thomas.

a pure home; and he was kept straight amid the temptations of artist life by the remembrance of the lessons of that home, and a voluntary obedience to the duties there impressed upon him. So that, as one of his friends says, when he became a man, Flandrin "only needed to be himself to be a Christian, just as to be an artist he only needed to follow his natural tastes and exercise his faculties." It was this perfect harmony between his characteristic talent and his habits of life, this entire conformity of the painter's inspirations with the principles and practice of the man, which have won Flandrin a claim to an altogether exceptional respect, and an unquestionable authority. Where so many other painters of sacred subjects under David, or earlier still, had but played a part skilfully, Flandrin devoted himself wholly to his art, because his work was as much the creation of his heart as of his mind. His piety in nowise dulled him to the delights of real beauty, any more than his zealous prosecution of art distracted him from metaphysical contemplation; and when in his early days at Rome, Flandrin wrote to his brother to send him some brushes and the Pensées de Pascal, he was unconsciously gathering up all the occupations, longings and passions of his life—a life divided between the need to paint sacred things and the no less imperative need to meditate upon and penetrate into their mysteries. Later on, when decorating the Church of Saint Paul at Nîmes, he inscribed the names of father and mother, sister and brother's wife and children, of all whom he had loved or lost, within a fold of the drapery of his figure of Christ at the top of the choir. It was not done as a token of his faith, or a profession of affection; the inscriptions are totally invisible, and moreover Flandrin only told one person what he had done, bidding him keep the secret. It was an *ex voto* intended for no eye save that of God, and it was as a prayer that his hand traced the words.

Probably the secret of Flandrin's influence as a man and as a painter may be traced to the same cause, what M. Delaborde calls his "thorough moral sincerity."

"Men believe in the artist's authority and his eloquence, because he himself believed in the things of which his pencil tells; they are touched with his emotion, infected as by a happy contagion with the Christian tenderness which breathes in all his works, because he felt it himself in every task, not by a mere effort of will or accidental act of intelligence, but through the wonted springs and innate cravings of his heart. Flandrin's thoughts followed readily and naturally into those ideal regions, those supernatural spheres where formerly Fra Angelico's spirit drank its inspirations; and when he covered the walls of churches with types of earthly renunciation or told the tale of heavenly mercy, when he depicted the beauty of self-abandonment to God, resignation and love in such unearthly purity, he seemed less to be fulfilling a task than obeying the laws of a natural vocation; rather to be embodying his familiar thoughts and memories than carrying out any formal plan."

"It was a new undertaking," M. Delaborde says elsewhere, "to combine the severity of religious thought with calm grace and peaceful ease of expression; just as it was in a fashion audacious—in practice anyhow most skilful—to unite the time-honoured traditions of beauty with conformity to what nature sets before our eyes; to embody on canvas the likeness of life's visible truths, together with the results of a training acquired in picture-galleries." This undertaking Flandrin achieved in his Dante, his Saint Clair, his picture of our Lord blessing the children; and while not forgetting the debt owed to other modern artists, among whom Orsel is chief—his aim being, as he said himself, "to baptize Greek art"—Flandrin carried out the principle and combined the higher tone of Christian realism with the recognised traditions of ancient art, believing heartily in both, and that more and more to the end of his life.

The episode of Roman life was finished; and returning to his native Lyons, Flandrin writes pathetically:

"I have done with my student life, and I must confess, that, in spite of the return to home and friends, it is with regret, a most keen regret, that I part from this period of my life. I might have been more fortunate perhaps, for eighteen months of fever do not tend to make one see things *en beau;* but I found so much not to be found elsewhere, so much to be deprived of, which seems intolerable as I look forward! It costs me more than I can say to part from it all; and, of course, just now the loss is felt at every turn, and the compensations are scarcely appreciable: perhaps later on I shall be more open to them." Probably most people who have spent any time, above all in study, at Rome, have more or less such cravings to return to its marvellous fascinations; certainly from the day of his departure in 1838 to the time he returned there—as it proved, to die—Flandrin longed after his beloved Rome; and in his letters, telling of worries, social conventionalities, and the like, from time to time a pathetic "O! for Rome once more!" creeps in.

But he was not a man to sit down and lose time over vain regrets or sentimentalities. The promised visit to his mother was paid on his way to Paris, where work, hard, resolute work, was Flandrin's deliberate aim and intention. He writes to his friend Ambroise Thomas:—

"LYONS, *Aug.* 9, 1838.

" . . . We gladly accept your proposal that we should come to you for the first few days. How pleasant it will be to talk! though indeed, as you say, we shall hardly know where to begin. But somehow I think we shall soon find ourselves in Rome! It is an endless subject, and one which I rejoice to associate so much with you. Coming back, after Florence, there are the Apennines, Bologna, and some other fine things; but how shall we find elsewhere the picturesque character of that wonderful land? Where else that rich, lovely vegetation, those woods of laurel and ilex, those magnificent pines, olives, orange and lemon trees, pomegranates, aloes? They are all replaced by willows and plane trees; the land is a marshy rice-field; everything is by rule and line! What a change! Nevertheless, after all this fastidious preparation, I could not cross the last Italian boundary with indifference. Among the glaciers at the top of the Simplon we said a loving and grateful farewell to Italy;—and indeed we have a large debt of happiness owing to her!"

The days of pedestrian journeys were over,—time was a more precious thing now to the artist brothers, and a diligence journey, much hindered by rains, brought them to Paris in the first days of September 1838. The first impression on his return was such as probably most of us have felt on re-entering a Northern town after sojourning in the South and amid the glowing tints of Italy. "There was the familiar Paris again, but with more noise, mud, smoke, and crowd than ever! For a moment it appalled me; it never had seemed so immense."

A weary time ensued, seeking an atelier. "Interminable running about in horrible weather after a studio. But at last we have ended in getting one in the Rue de Lille. It is fairly good, but very dear, although cheaper than the rest. Seven hundred francs! and then, besides that, we have to think about our own quarters, for we are still with Thomas."

After installing himself in this studio, Flandrin and his brother Paul returned to Lyons for a month, finally settling in Paris in November, whence he writes to his mother:—

"*Nov.* 30, 1838.—Monday was a dismal day; we were leaving you for a long time, and the rain, which lasted nearly all day, would not allow us to go on deck, and we had to stay below till we reached Châlons, at half-past nine in the evening. There we took the diligence, which was full, and in the *coupé* between us we had an Englishman, who proved very agreeable. At ten o'clock, final start; but our pace was that of the tortoise, and the climax was, that at Avallon, on Tuesday evening, there were no horses to be had at the *messagerie*. So we waited five hours in the middle of the street, until at last, in despair, when it was past midnight, we decided to go and knock up the mayor, the head of the police, the *juge de paix*, and all the authorities of the place! Their united efforts at last took effect with the postmaster, who would not give us horses because the officials had not applied to him first of all. At last we got off,—rain, fog, everything horrible—to Paris, where, instead of arriving, as promised, on Wednesday evening, we did not find ourselves till seven o'clock on Thursday morning. We were tired, but would not go to bed. We went to the Musée (Louvre), and thence to our studio, where we found everything in order."

Hippolyte Flandrin's picture of our Lord with the little ones was in the Louvre, and, as we have seen, he was anxious to sell it; but his artist's pride had some severe struggles to endure. Soon after his return to Paris he writes to his brother Auguste:—

"PARIS, *Dec.* 3, 1838.

"I want you to do me a service, into which I know you will throw yourself zealously. This is it. Yesterday I was going to the Ministère de l'Intérieur to see M. Dumont,[1] to whom I attribute the success of my picture with the Minister, when it came into my head to go first to M. Gatteaux, who said, 'Well, I have seen

[1] Chef du Bureau des Beaux Arts.

Dumont; he told me that your picture is sold, and that they will give you three thousand francs!' So far from being overcome by this generosity, I made a grimace which I had to hide as best I could; and I asked M. Gatteaux what was to be done with my picture. He said nothing was known, but they thought of sending it to some country museum. I thanked him for the information and retired, postponing my visit to M. Dumont out of prudence. I was prepared for something of this sort, but one is always taken by surprise when a thing actually happens. If I did not expect a very magnificent price, at least I reckoned on a more honourable position. But you see it is a great favour;—they don't suppose I could possibly refuse such a thing! They don't know what to do with it, but nevertheless they buy it and rid one of it! Oh, how I should like to say 'It is sold at a higher price!' So please see Petrus, and ascertain what chance there is of his plan for getting the picture bought for Saint Louis being carried out. Nevertheless, one must act prudently; for I must confess my object would be to show that I have other resources, and I must further confess that I would rather sell it for less here if I had been given a place in a Paris church or gallery. I think, dear old fellow, that you will understand. See to it, but keep my letter and its drops of vinegar to yourself!"

"PARIS, *Dec.* 7, 1838.

"Thanks, dear Auguste, for what you have done. I shall not, however, go to M. Roland; it is impossible for me to make such a proposition myself. Moreover, M. Gatteaux says that these gentlemen at the Ministère would be charmed at my refusal, and that it would be tantamount to scratching my own name off the list for future work. So you see I must end by doing as they would have me, which is rather hard, for at that rate, considering Paris expenses, it would be impossible for me to do another work on the same scale. They grind painting down to the mere trade level by depriving one of the possibilities of progress. You see I was not far wrong in my judgment beforehand of the world we have to do with. As for you, work away, and make the most of what you have got down there. Paris is not so beautiful after all when you are in it! But your picture! your picture!"

"PARIS, *Jan.* 6, 1839.

"Thanks, my dear Auguste, for the advice you give me in the kindness of your heart;—but, but—oh, what a lot of buts! As to going to see the '*gros bonnets*,' I assure you that is quite too great a hardship. Since I came here I have tried to do it, and if it were to go on I could not stand up against it at all. Oh, for my dear Rome! But here to be treated with so little consideration, and to be obliged as a matter of calculation to thank people for the miserable offers they make one—if indeed they do as much as that, for they think themselves conferring such a favour that they dispose of one's work without so much as condescending to say they have bought it! You didn't know that they were going to send my picture to Fécamp, a thing which M. Dumont happily put a stop to. . . . I went to see the Préfet a fortnight ago; but between ourselves be it said, I determined not to go there again in a hurry, not being accustomed to be received in such a way, that is to say, so drily, with the most marked coldness, leaving me to say what I would, without a word as to what he had seen or had not seen. In spite of this I invited him as well as I could to come and see my picture and Paul's. He could not promise,—said that he would try, etc. etc., and here is a fortnight gone by and no Préfet. I have seen a great many people who might have been useful to me, but most of them think it enough if they are civil. There was no one but good M. Foyatier,[1] who was excited at the idea of my picture going for three thousand francs. He talked, brought people to see it, did everything in his power, but . . . Well! patience. Only work is out of the question with this perpetual running about, and one is

[1] The sculptor whose example and pleadings had first led Flandrin's parents to consent to his studying art.

decidedly worth more than the other, for some people, —and it seems that I am one of them,—never can make much of that trade!

"One thing in your letter displeases me very much: I mean the discouraged tone in which you speak of your picture.[1] It vexes me exceedingly, for I was so full of hope. It is so well begun, that one might almost consider it done. Now then, once for all, do what you can, and I shall be satisfied. . . . Pray, dear old fellow, work away, and I will answer for your success. Paul's picture improves daily, and what I have done to mine has had a good result too. Take good care of our dear mother. Oh, if we could but have her here, how happy we should be, for, to tell the truth, we are not over-cheerful in this Paris, with all its absurd grandeur, where one doesn't come at one's friends as one would like. Thomas himself we see but rarely; between Desgoffe and us there lies about a *lieue* and a half, and inasmuch as directly rain or fog come Paris turns into a pond, more or less deep, we cannot pay one another many visits. . . . Don't go and fancy, after all, that I am out of heart. When I have thoroughly set to work, when I have begun another picture, it will be all right. The thing which really weighs me down is the rent I have on my hands."

[1] This was a picture of Savonarola preaching in San Miniato, which he exhibited in Paris in 1840, and which is now in the Musée at Lyons.

"PARIS, *Feb.* 13, 1839.

"Sometimes I forget myself, and date my letters from Rome, though, certainly, there are plenty of things to remind me that I am no longer there! The *Salon* (Exhibition) draws near. To-morrow we send in our pictures. God grant that Paul's pictures may be well placed, for I think if they are seen they will be successful. We are working hard, but with constant interruptions; for we have a constant stream of visitors—sometimes as many as twenty or thirty persons. Just conceive, with short, dark days, and all the visits we are obliged to pay, how much time is lost! We have not been able to stay at home one evening since we got here. All this is a matter of constraint and necessity, and without exaggeration we have only once been able to get an hour's walk—whenever we go out it is sure to be on unavoidable business. I don't know whether I shall get accustomed to this kind of life, but just at present it wearies me horribly. O Rome! Rome!

"As for you, it seems to me that you are working very hard. So much the better, but you don't tell me about other things. Are you thinking of marrying? It would be reasonable. And have you done as I advised you, and seen a little more of the world this winter? If you hide yourself, my dear fellow, you will not be found out. . . . . I must tell you, just for yourself and mama, that there is an idea of giving me a chapel in Saint Severin—very bad pay as I hear, but it is an opening for doing something really good, and just now that is what I must think most about. I am working at compositions for it, and in a month's time I fancy it will be decided. Till then don't let us be too confident, but it would be delightful."

*To M. Eugène Roger, at the Academy of France at Rome.*

"PARIS, *March* 11, 1839.

" . . . . As to the Salon, March 2, at eleven o'clock, we got in with the stream of the crowd. The opening had been delayed a day in consequence of the quantity of works sent in. It was splendid weather, and the great salon was dazzling. First of all we saw M. Vernet occupying the whole of one side with three pictures of the *Prise de Constantine.* At the first glance I was taken by a certain life about them, and by the clear, simple way in which the action is given, but go into details, and they lose considerably. Then come Decamp's pictures, which strike me as better than anything of his I have seen before. I can hardly describe them, as there are eleven, and it would be too long a story. On the other side of the great salon, rather too high unfortunately, comes Paul's great landscape, which is greatly improved, and which, to my mind, is the most classical in the whole Exhibition, although Aligny, Edouard Bertin, Marilhat, Corot, etc., have pictures in it. There is also a Saint Luke painting the Blessed Virgin in the great saloon by Ziegler, which does not please me immensely, but in which one is forced to recognise power and repose, which separate it in a measure from the otherwise universal confusion and chaos.

"Except the pictures I have mentioned, the grand salon is full of the worst things in the Exhibition. Apparently out of consideration for my unlucky cartoon, they wouldn't put it in such company; it is in the gallery where the Davids are. That might have been all very well if it had been at a reasonable height, but they have perched it right up atop, with a window above it, so that the daylight makes a sort of frame to it, and a window opposite, like a mirror. Indeed, I wish it were still less seen, and then people would not try to form any opinion of it up there!

"Then, by way of portraits, we have all the Royal Family, by Winterhalter, but they are not very remarkable. There is a picture by one Leullier, of the Christians thrown to wild beasts in the Coliseum. Perhaps the subject is not particularly well chosen, but the animals are drawn admirably, and their action wonderful; it is full of energy. Desgoffe has several good pictures, but, like Paul's four others, they are villanously hung. Signol has a picture for Versailles, Saint Bernard preaching the Crusades; and Bézard too has a picture, which is a good composition and well conceived, but the details are entirely study, and I think there are certain points which can only be attained in the actual presence of nature.

"At the end of the great gallery Scheffer exhibits five pictures, which touch one another, and make a sort of background to each other in a very clever way. To my mind they are full of delicate feeling, but at the same time a little bit *pleureur*. The colouring wants power; it is simple, but rather flat and smooth. Nevertheless, M. Scheffer is supreme in the salon, as may be supposed. As for the rest, *ma foi!* I have nothing to say about them, except that I don't know what they are at! . . .

"I must tell you that, amid all the misfortunes of my picture, it has got a happier prospect in store. They have promised me that, after the Exhibition, it shall go for a time to the Luxembourg, and after that to Lyons. Just now there is a question of my painting a chapel in Saint Severin. If that might come to pass I should be very happy, although I am told beforehand that it will not pay, and that it will have to be well and quickly done. I have often thought, my dear Roger, of taking a studio (of pupils), as you used to advise at Naples. Some fifteen young men have already applied to me, but, not knowing M. Ingres' mind on the subject, I refused them. Some however persist, and I have determined to write to M. Ingres about it. As I wrote to him a few days ago, I enclose a note for him to you. If you talk it over together, and he does not answer at once, I wish you would do so yourself. You know all I think about the matter, and the reasons which have made me refuse hitherto. So, if M. Ingres should talk to you about it, tell him everything, for above all things I would not have him think one presumptuous and self-assuming."

M. Ingres heartily urged Flandrin to open a studio for pupils, and in the month of April 1839 he wrote to his brother Auguste that he was preparing to do so, and looked forward with pleasure to extending his master's school; but he never carried out the intention, and six months later he says in a letter to Auguste that Madame George Sand was anxious he should take her son as a private pupil, but that he had refused, for want of proper accommodation.

The picture Flandrin exhibited at this Exhibition, of our Lord blessing little children, met with very great admiration among his brethren of the art. Among these Ary Scheffer was prominent. He had been one of the first to visit the picture while yet in the painter's studio, and, regardless of his great name and undoubted successes, he exclaimed, "Why is it not given to me to follow confidently as you do in this track! Why did I not acquire a teaching such as you have had, but which it is too late for me to seek! You can express what you feel as you will; you know, and I do not know. My pictures only let intentions peep out without affirming anything, and your pictures prove it to me by force of contrast." Nor were these mere words, for Scheffer studied Flandrin's works carefully, often took counsel with him, and to the end treated him with a deference which caused much more perplexity than pride to the younger artist. Paul Delaroche was equally liberal in sympathy and applause, and M. Gatteaux exerted himself to obtain scope for the exercise of the talents he appreciated. It was through him that Flandrin was commissioned first to paint the Chapel of St. John in Saint Severin, and later, the Choir of Saint Germain des Prés. Conscious of the truth of his art principles, and standing emphatically by them throughout, there was no particle of self-assumption or vanity in Flandrin's mind. Whatever success he obtained he always attributed to the teaching of his beloved master, to whom, up to the last days of his life, he showed the same deference expressed in the first year of his studentship, the same gratitude "for one I can never admire or love sufficiently." And this exceeding modesty and freedom from self-assumption or conceit drew men to Flandrin in a wondrous way. "Completely without self-confidence as he was, timid and shrinking to the last degree when encountering praise or having to go through some worldly ceremonial" (so writes a friend), "how well he understood reassuring and convincing any one who stood in need of counsel, encouragement, or sympathy!" In all dealings with other men, Flandrin set himself entirely aside, even among those who were unquestionably his inferiors: whether in public or private he always avoided everything tending to bring himself forward, and seemed to dread being made prominent as much as most men dread being overlooked. Not that he did not desire to win the prizes of his art, but it was without self-consciousness or vanity—for the art's sake, not for his own; and to see Paul successful was a greater happiness than to be successful himself. Yet he was not other than alive to what he considered justice.

After the Exhibition of 1839 he writes to his mother and Auguste: "Paul has had great success; to my mind his landscape is the best in the Exhibition, and fortunately I am not singular in my opinion. . . . The prizes have been awarded. The *croix d'honneur* to MM. X., a *mitraille* of medals to MM. So-and-so. M. Paul Flandrin, whose picture has been deservedly noticed and admired, has permission to take it home again, a favour he will know how to justify by renewed efforts. M. Hippolyte Flandrin's picture has been bought, as you know, by the Ministère de l'Intérieur. It was destined for the Luxembourg Gallery, then for that of Lyons; but in consideration of the legitimate success it has obtained its destination is changed, and it is to be sent to Lisieux, a town of eight or ten thousand inhabitants, with a Musée already containing two pictures and three casts, and where the Municipal Council may be inclined to vote a grant for the construction of a hall fit to contain these objects of art. *Voilà!* But all the same, one must be resigned, and reckon one's-self fortunate, and seek in one's own conscience a reward which I know is worth more than that of the world. Anyhow, that is what one ought to do, but it is difficult. Sometimes one lets off a strain of uncontrollable indignation. Adieu, dear old fellow; let us always do our best, and then—*arrive que pourra!*"

And again:—

"PARIS, *May* 17, 1839.

"Now the Exhibition is over, and between ourselves I may tell you that your two brothers were of the best, but there was not the smallest offer from the Ministry or the King's household. Nevertheless, they buy the most rubbishy works, and shower prizes, *croix d'honneur* and the like, upon them. That's what comes of being well backed, which is very far from being our case. We know a great many people, but no one speaks on our behalf, and as to asking for myself it is a thing I could not do. But remember, please, this grumbling is only between ourselves. I always do and always shall tell you whatever I think, and perhaps there may be some hope yet. I should specially have liked to see poor Paul's picture sold. If you had seen it among all the rest, there really was no comparison. All artists did him justice, but the administration is not *connaisseuse.*"

Among the friends who appeared in Paris now, the brothers were pleased to see General Paultre de Lamothe again,—the same good soldier who was commanding at Lyons in the days of their boyhood, and who used to take so much interest in the military sketches of the "petits Flandrin," now, as he prophesied, become "real artists." After one of his never-forgotten affectionate visits to his mother, Flandrin returned in July 1839 to Paris. "The rheumatism," he announces, "took its departure on the way, and I must tell you that I behaved very well, for though I had left all I love I was not too sad. I should like to know if little mother has been as good, and whether I have to scold or to thank her! Meanwhile I embrace her with all my heart. I found a heap of letters here—some asking me to dinner, some to dance! and one telling you, Paul, that your picture is come back from Orléans, that is to say, unsold as before. . . . . I saw my chapel this morning. . . . . Work hard, Paul, and don't you, Auguste, lose any of your zeal. Dear mama, you will pray for all three!"

Paul remained a little longer with their mother, and while at Lyons, he received dismal news of his pictures from Hippolyte.

" . . . . My dear Paul,—I must tell you what is not pleasant; but after all we are men, and so hard enough (*coriaces*) to bear worse than this. I told you that your picture had come back from Orléans, the one sent to Nantes is also returned, and finally the big one is not more fortunate. . . . *Ci vuole pazienza!* . . . . Dear old fellow, you remember that on leaving Lyons I regretted not having been able to go *up there* to our dear father. Well, it worries me. If you could go with Auguste and say a little prayer for us both, it would be a good thing. If it is possible, please do so, dear Paul. But if you cannot, don't tell Auguste to go alone; he has suffered too much already."

Paul rejoined his brother, "and everybody says, '*Voilà le Flandrin tout entier!*'" The two artists established themselves in No. 14 Rue de l'Abbaye, and there Flandrin continued to live until the final journey to Rome, in 1863, where he ended his days.

Hippolyte's letters to Auguste continue to urge study. "Work, raise the tone of your mind, think of all that is beautiful and expansive, and if you can, read. I shall for ever sing the same song; one must renew, revive one's ideas. Forgive me for perpetually bothering you, but I am too thoroughly convinced of the value of the advice not to repeat it continually. Homer, Plutarch, Tacitus, Virgil, and such inspire the beauty which we love."

The commission for Saint Severin had been given to Flandrin, and at the end of the year he writes:—

"PARIS, *Dec.* 23, 1839.

"My cartoons occupy me greatly with all the necessary study for them, to say nothing of all the painters and masons one has to direct. All this too in about five hours' daylight, and such daylight too! Paris is a gutter—a very swamp—through which one must paddle to pay visits, and comply with the exigencies of this ridiculous world. (Dear Rome, where art thou?) Oh, how often I get into a rage, and would fain get rid of all this world's nonsense! But one must live. In this famous Paris people won't hunt you out, you must appear, and very often the most impudent fares best. I have not yet been able to return to the Ministère. I cannot forget all the proceedings about my picture, and nothing short of necessity will take me there again. I know people who are quite content to spend a couple of hours every Thursday in M. Cavé's antechamber, and who accept his bad humour as well as his good humour; but I am sure you would not like it any better than I do. Poor Paul is still less of a visitor, and still less fortunate. Neither portraits nor pictures, nothing befalls him, not the smallest bit of provender, and consequently it is impossible for him to follow your advice about laying by. As to me, I can do no better. We shall soon both be driven to our last resources, for they will advance me nothing for the Chapel until the cartoons are done, and even then the money paid in will be swallowed up at once by the work-people, who are already putting in their claims."

Hippolyte's watchful interest for Auguste did not flag. He writes:—

"PARIS, *Feb.* 5, 1840.

" . . . . In your last letter you speak of not coming to Paris. I cannot consent to that. How can you profit by the Exhibition? You must see yourself and others there, or else not work at all for exhibitions, as it would be quite a mistake to judge yourself according to the favour or rejection of the public. You must study yourself there. It is all very well to say that you are held fast by your pupils. You might easily leave them for a fortnight, and let us enjoy a glimpse of our brother."

"*Feb.* 6, 1840.—This evening late we received your pictures, all arrived in good health. You can imagine our impatience unpacking them, but I should have liked you to witness our joy in recognising a quantity of delightful things. To-day, before it was light, we were at your pictures, and according to your permission we have rubbed, glazed, softened, deepened little odd touches, all things which you would have done yourself if you had had a week to spare. But I tell you that we were very much satisfied. You should have seen Louis' delight."

Louis Lamothe was first a pupil of Auguste, who sent him in November 1839 to his brother's care, and to the end Lamothe remained the devoted friend and assistant of Hippolyte Flandrin. Auguste's picture was duly sent to the Exhibition.

"PARIS, *March* 6, 1840.

"When we get you we will tell you the faults we find with your picture. Meanwhile all we can say is, that it has pleased us very much, as well as many others, artists and friends, for I must tell you that it appeared in a sort of Exhibition we had at home for a few days.

"The Salon opened yesterday, and I want to tell

you that you are very well placed. You are seen, and gain more than you lose. So all is for the best, and it comforts us a little for the horrible place assigned to our poor Paul's four pictures; but he is very brave, and does not allow himself to be cast down, and I have a firm conviction that he will soon rise, as to talent, above those highest placed and most thought of. I am sorry that you can't come now, because naturally I lose a certain time through the Exhibition, which we could have spent together, whereas by and bye, when you come, I shall be in full chapel work, and as they hurry me it will be difficult to leave it."

Flandrin's wish that his mother should come to Paris was fulfilled this year, and it is touching to find him making little arrangements for the comfort of her journey,—with daughter-like care, begging her to keep her feet warm, planning to meet her at the bureau on her arrival, trying to make her comfortable in the little room, doing his best to amuse her and be her companion, although so pressed with work that, as he tells Auguste in a letter of April 1st, he "has not a moment of rest, really not time to eat."

Flandrin had always been subject to a squint, and when the supposed discovery was made, that by means of an operation severing a particular muscle in the eye this deformity could be rectified, he readily consented to undergo the treatment. At the moment the operation appeared to be successful, but his eyes soon recovered their normal condition, and he squinted as much as ever, with the undesirable addition of a rapid failure of sight in his right eye, which had always been weaker than the other. Before long this right eye became perfectly useless, and for years all Flandrin's work was done under the difficulty of such an imperfect sight. He writes to Auguste :—

"PARIS, *Feb.* 19, 1841.

"Tell mama that my eye is mending, and will soon be well. People here have been so wonderfully kind, they have taken as much interest in it as if it were an important matter. It got known, and the house was always full of visitors, whose sympathy I fully appreciate. . . . Adieu—I am forbidden to tire myself, which does not coincide with all my business, for I never was so pressed."

"*Feb.* 24, 1841.—I know you would be pleased at the success of the operation. . . . Unfortunately the last few days there has been some going back. At times the eye returns to its old position, but they hope that as it recovers strength it will keep right. I have suffered enough to deserve thorough success ; and the anxiety caused by this little fluctuation was very keen at first, but we must bear what cannot be helped, and trust everything to God's Grace."

At this time Flandrin undertook to paint the great hall of the Château de Dampierre, and it was when about to go thither that he wrote urging Auguste and his mother to come and live with him and Paul in Paris,—all the tender consideration for her comfort and desire for his brother's advancement, which were so marked a part of his character, taking part in his arguments.

"We want you. Is it not a trial for those who love one another to live apart, perpetually sighing after reunion? Do what you will, our dear mother must have long seasons of solitude when you are at work; but among the three we could give her more constant companionship—if not one, it could be another. Moreover, when I look at your portrait of M. Desguidi, I say that it is a pity to hide away such talents, which would increase here more rapidly and more surely, besides finding better opportunity for coming to light. Think of all this, but don't be too long thinking. Half one's life is spent in projects! . . ."

In April 1841 Flandrin writes in high spirits about his work, though so hurried and pressed about the wall paintings at Dampierre, that he had to leave Paris just as the Exhibition opened, and as the public was admitted to see his Chapel in Saint Severin. He and Louis Lamothe worked from six in the morning to six in the evening; but Flandrin never shrank from work, though before he had finished his paintings at Dampierre, he fell ill from over-pressure, and from the bad air he breathed, shut up in a close hall with a quantity of other painters at work. The Chapel met with great admiration, and, what Flandrin valued more than the approbation of Prefect, Municipal Council and Institut,—Varcollier, whose judgment M. Ingres esteemed highly, wrote a highly commendatory critique of it. A further testimony to his merits appeared in his nomination as a member of the Legion d'Honneur, and the man's simple, unselfish character comes out in the way he announces this fact to his mother and brother.

"PARIS, *June* 24, 1841.

"I lose no time in telling you the news which M. Ingres has brought to celebrate your fête and mine. The King appoints me a Member of the Legion of Honour, and I am happy to see the pleasure it gives to our friends. I am certain of yours, and that of our relations and friends at Lyons, which greatly increases the value of the honour conferred on me. I heartily long for the same to be granted to my dear Auguste and Paul, who only need full opening to show their talent, to obtain their deserts. . . ."

Flandrin's stedfast mind on religious subjects is

put forth in a plain practical way, when replying to his brother Auguste, who had asked his advice on the subject of matrimony.

"PARIS, *July* 18, 1841.

"With respect to . . . believe me, even if a man has allowed his religion to grow slack in his heart for long, it is dangerous to become united with a woman of a lower standard. Those differences which seem unimportant at first may by and bye become causes of disunion, especially where there are children, and without wishing to hinder or weaken the religious instruction they receive, father or mother find themselves, if not condemned, at least accused by their young ones. And besides, you know as well as I do that it is in religion only (we have a beautiful illustration of it in our mother) that we can find any real strength amid trials and sorrows. If a man feels this sincerely and deeply, what a misery not to share the conviction fully with her whom he loved! Consider all this, my dear fellow, and think it well over."

And a little later he says on the same subject: "I want you to have a wife who loves you heartily, and above all of a high tone of mind. That seems to me the most important thing to be wished, for it includes what may be called the ordinary gifts, those everyday virtues which affect the happiness of life at every hour."

Apparently the advice was followed, for Auguste Flandrin did not marry. Hippolyte spent part of that autumn at Lyons, and wrote of his brother's works as advancing greatly in breadth and solidity. Returning to Paris, he continued actively to promote Auguste's professional interests, getting some of his portraits (which the younger brother criticises freely though lovingly) into the Exhibition of 1842, where his own picture of "Saint Louis dictant ses Établissements,"[1] was exhibited; and continuing to urge the plan already proposed, for the whole family to live together in Paris, where he tells his mother he now has a housekeeper to cook and take care of things, living quite like "gens établis." His affectionate heart seems to have craved for his mother's presence. "May God long preserve you to your children," he writes to her, "and render you happy in their love. I trust my father sees and knows it all; he knows that we do not forget him. His memory is precious and honourable to us—happy the children who can keep such memories of their parents. Dearest mother, I know that these remembrances do not sadden you—they are ever with you, and it is so comfortable to talk of what one loves." And to Auguste he says, "May God preserve our mother to us, and allow us to share in your care for her. May the reunion I have

[1] Now in the Palais du Sénat.

so long desired come to pass, so that we may all enjoy one another for such time as is given us. Time does indeed pass very quickly, and I regret above all not to be living for those I love best."

Letter after letter is full of the like affectionate urgency. In spite of pressing work, Dampierre was finished at the end of May 1842, with a last most fatiguing effort in painting the ceiling (for Flandrin suffered cruelly from rheumatism); a portrait of Mademoiselle Delessert, which he says "frightens me horribly;" and preparation for his great frescoes in Saint Germain des Prés, a work just entrusted to him. His tender heart was sorely touched by the sad death of the Duc d'Orléans, July 13, 1842, which, he says, had thrown all Paris into gloom and mourning, and more than ever he longed to be united to his own dearly-loved ones. That was the last letter he ever wrote to his brother Auguste, who was suddenly seized with brain-fever, from which he did not recover. The instant Hippolyte heard of his brother's illness, he left everything, and started for Lyons, arriving there August 23rd. Auguste recognised his brothers, and showed signs of pleasure at seeing them, but could not speak, and in a few days he died, lovingly tended to the last by his two brothers and his mother. Flandrin writes to a friend:—

"LYONS, *Sept.* 1, 1842.

"It is all over, and this morning we laid him in his last earthly resting-place. From the time we got here we watched the disease advancing steadily, but still there was some hope, and to the end everything possible was done, but vainly. The last agony began about five o'clock on Tuesday morning, and he was gone by ten o'clock. We closed his eyes, and after a loving embrace, we left him, to devote ourselves to our poor mother. Her resignation is very beautiful, but it is a heavy blow. . . . Our dear brother's death has been generally and deeply felt in the town. Almost every one of any position attended the funeral this morning, and this last proof of respect and affection was very soothing to us. You knew him, and I am sure you will regret him. *Nous étions si bien à trois!* Now we seem to have lost so much. So we must draw all the closer to our friends. . . ."

And to Ambroise Thomas, Flandrin writes mournfully :—"Now that the first stunning grief is past, if you only knew how deep our grief is! Everything seems to feed and increase it. It was so good to be three, and when there are only two, one seems so near being left alone! Sad indeed for the one left last! Forgive this outpour of weakness, but there it is, in the bottom of my heart. The one who seemed so strong, so full of life, has been taken so suddenly from us. On the very first day he said that he felt himself taken for death. Our poor mother feels this severe blow very keenly, but with great courage. We must not be ungrateful to God, but thank Him for sparing her to us."

His letters of that autumn to his mother are naturally full of the beloved one who had gone from them, and the tenderness of his consolations to the bereaved mother are very touching. Hippolyte was himself about to carry out the good advice he had given to Auguste, and to unite himself to a wife who was likeminded and who would strengthen him in all that was good. His mother's approbation was anxiously and dutifully sought when he resolved to make Mademoiselle Aimée Ancelot his wife.

"We rejoice in your consent, which we hold to be an indispensable blessing in so weighty a matter. I shall take the good tidings this day to her family, thereby adding to the kindness with which they receive me—all are prepared to love you. The more I see of them the happier I am. . . . We hope to be married about Easter. Your presence cannot be dispensed with, indeed we would willingly wait to have you present. I am grieved to have to write so hurriedly, for on such an occasion there is very much I should like to say. But to be brief, dearest mother, I will only say that I accept this great happiness with trust in God and in my good intentions. Your prayers cannot fail to bring us a blessing. May the event bring some gladness to your poor heart, so sorely tried, yet still so fresh and warm and loving. On Ash-Wednesday we heard Mass for our dear Auguste. It was six months from the day, and we assisted, feeling our loss as freshly as in the first days. Pray continually, dearest mother, for him and for us."

"The more I know of her who is about to be my wife," he writes to Ambroise Thomas, "the more I love her, and rejoice;" and on May 10th, the day before the wedding, he writes to the same friend:—"I am very happy, I am just winning my prize. . . . I find even more than I could have dared to hope for! She is charming, so gentle and tender. Rejoice with me! Please come rather early, for the organist is not in Paris, and if you come at a quarter to twelve or half-past eleven, you can feel your ground. Try to remember some of the beautiful bits we used to be so fond of, the *Ave verum*, etc."

The marriage took place May 11, 1843, and Madame Flandrin must have felt that, as Hippolyte said, she had gained another child, rather than lost her son, or his devoted tender care and affection. "Your *trois petits* love you dearly;" he used to write, ever associating Aimée as well as Paul in all his tenderness to his mother. He was occupied from May 1842 to the end of 1844 with the decoration of the sanctuary of Saint Germain des Prés, paintings in which the large subjects consist of the Entry into Jerusalem and our Lord bearing His Cross on Calvary, as also of figures on the left side representing Faith, Hope, Charity, and Patience, Saint Germain and S. Doctrovée (the first Abbot of Saint Germain des Prés) receiving the model of the church from Childebert and Ultrogoth; and on the right side, Justice, Prudence, Temperance and Strength, with Saint Vincent, the Pope Alexander III., the Abbé Morard, Saint Benedict and King Robert. The paintings in the choir were of a later date, 1846 to 1848, and those in the nave were in progress from 1855 to 1861.

Flandrin's heart was in his work; he repeatedly thanks God for having given him the opportunity of devoting himself to religious painting, and the tenor of his thoughts, always calmly devout, seems to have become increasingly so under the influence of his sacred task.

"Just now as I went to work," he writes to his mother, "I begged the Blessed Virgin to go and see you in your dark little corner by the clock, where I fancy you must be very *triste* in this bad weather. I am sure she will have given heed to my prayer. She must love you,—you are so good and kind and patient, and you bend your will so gently and submissively to God's Will. I only wish we could imitate you as much as we love you!" Among other works finished at this time (1844-5) was a picture painted for the Prince de Berghes, for his mortuary chapel at Saint Martory, near Saint Gaudens (Haute Garonne). It was to be a Mater dolorosa, and Flandrin took as the motto of his picture the words of Jeremiah, "O all ye that pass by behold and see if there be any sorrow like unto my sorrow."[1] He described it himself as "the Blessed Virgin at the foot of the Cross, offering the instruments of our Saviour's Passion to Christians as a subject of meditation." This was painted during the cold dark days which would not allow of his working at Saint Germain des Prés. Perhaps the best tribute that could have been paid to this picture was involuntarily offered by the Queen Marie Amélie, whose mother's heart, still bleeding from the awfully sudden death of the Duc d'Orléans, was transfixed by the beauty and sympathy of Flandrin's representation of the Mother of Sorrows, so that on first seeing the picture in the Exhibition of 1845, she burst into a flood of tears, and stood gazing in rapt earnestness before it. It was no mere artistic effect that could do this, but the painter's life was in keeping with the subjects on which he worked. He

[1] Lamentations i. 12.

does not say much in his letters upon religious subjects, but there is an undercurrent of practical devotion and serious thought which betokens the constant influence religion had over all he did. That his duties were regularly attended to, and as no mere form, such sentences in his letters as the following show :—" *April* 1, 1845.—Yesterday we all three kept our Easter (avons fait nos pâques) together, and consequently together prayed for you. It is a great happiness when fulfilling so holy a duty to see those one loves beside one, though, alas ! they were not all there !"

A fresh source of happiness was opened this year to Flandrin, when he became a father; and an enthusiastic admirer of his baby son he was from the first. He writes to his own mother :—

"PARIS, *Oct.* 9, 1845.

" Dearest Mama,—I have good news for you. A little man came into the world last night. He and his mother are doing well, the doctor is satisfied, and I leave you to imagine whether I am. I know how glad you will be. . . . Oh the delight of hearing the first cry of this little cherished being, so beloved already ! You, dearest mother, know what the delight is, and I can see you now thanking God for having given it to your children. Naturally we think the little darling charming, and really, prejudice apart, I think he is much prettier than most children of his age. We dwell upon that, because there is nothing else to be expected of him now, but later on we must hope to find that he has a good heart, and to train it well. I mean him to love everything good and beautiful; in short, I intend him to be a thorough good fellow, able to love and worthy of being loved."

And again :—

"PARIS, *Dec.* 15, 1845.

"I must tell you, dear mother, that our dear child gets on wonderfully. He has grown so as to surprise everybody, and his intelligence is beginning to wake up; he follows one with his eyes, and gives one such pretty little smiles when one talks to him; he listens with a kind of attention, sometimes answering with the sweetest little cooing. When he laughs, it is perfectly delicious, and like a sunbeam lighting up the house. Of course I see it all with a father's eyes—somewhat prejudiced—but nevertheless, dear mother, everybody thinks your little grandson very charming. We will try to make him grow up good . . . . We have made the little one kiss this letter—so he sends you his own kiss."

"PARIS, *Feb.* 20, 1846.

" . . . . I wish I could send you a portrait of your

little grandson, with the gracious smile which is so bewitching, but, alas! everything of that sort is so changeable, so fugitive, so bad to catch! . . . . Oh how I wish you could watch our darling child's growth, his good looks, his fun, and his attempts to chatter! If you could only see his delight on seeing us when he wakes up—how he flutters legs and arms all at once, like a little bird that fain would fly, if only its feathers were not still too short! . . . I send you two or three scratches made of the little fellow, but though they are like after a fashion, they are quite without his life and grace."

At the end of a technical letter to his friend Lacuria, we find the admiring father reporting "*notre petit* to be a model for Raffaele's beautiful children," and moreover gifted with a laugh quite superior to ordinary babies, able to listen with intelligent attention; in short, altogether a wondrous piece of babydom! Remembering those early days of privation and discomfort in Paris, so bravely borne by the artist brothers, it is pleasant to find them leading a life, unexciting and hard-working enough certainly, but comfortable and happy, as well-filled and industrious.

"PARIS, *Jan.* 10, 1847.

"This is how our winter days are spent. Up at

eight o'clock—not very early to be sure, but I must tell the truth. So—up at eight o'clock—quick, a cup of milk, and then we are in the studio till eleven, when real breakfast comes. At half-past eleven quickly back to the studio, where we work till five o'clock. Then by wolf's light (entre chien et loup) a run on the Quai Voltaire, if the weather permits, which it does not always. Dinner at six. In the middle of the repast the heir is brought in and takes his place between papa and mama, in his high chair. He coaxes us a great deal, eats a little, and amuses us endlessly. After that come games and rolling on the carpet, then he grows sleepy and is undressed, making his round of kisses, and so disappears. Father and uncle then set to work at drawings, compositions, reading or writing connected with their work, till their time for getting sleepy comes too! Meanwhile, after her child's toilette, and after having mended stockings, gowns and caps, my dear wife sometimes goes to the piano and practises for a bit, which is always a pleasure to us. And so my days go by. . . ."

Flandrin had now no need to look out anxiously for work—his name was well known, and as he says himself, he was overwhelmed with commissions, although refusing numbers, and he only wished for ten hands! His reputation was fast making him a lion in the world, and as such he found himself sought and fêted. His account of an evening at the Duc de Nemours', given to his mother, is written with all the simplicity of his early days in the garret au 5$^{eme}$:— "Aimée told you, dearest mama, that I had been asked to Court. Was not that something wonderful? Nevertheless it is quite true. I went, and was very much interested. It was a concert at the Duc de Nemours'. I made myself smart—black coat, white waistcoat, white tie, black trousers, silk stockings, varnished boots, but woe's me! going up the staircase, I perceived that every one in sight was in knee-breeches! It was very alarming, especially as there is a much stricter etiquette at the Duke's salon than in the King's. However, on I went, and in a few minutes I had the comfort of seeing one, two, three, and in course of time a good many trousers to keep me in countenance. The Duke and Duchess de Nemours made a round of the salons, speaking to their guests, and trying to say something courteous to every one. I pitied them with all my heart, for it really is a hard task. A little later the King and Queen of the Belgians, the Duke and Duchess d'Aumale and de Montpensier arrived: the ladies went into the concert-room, the princes stayed among the men, talking with ministers, peers, deputies, savants, literary men and artists. The Duc de Montpensier, to whom I was presented, came and thanked me for a drawing I made some months ago for his album, referred to several of my works with a most winning grace, and finally (what quite won my heart) asked after my brother and his 'beautiful pictures.' The Duchesse de Nemours too was very gracious. About midnight the concert came to an end, the royalties retired, the crowd dispersed quietly, and I came home to my wife, and tried to tell her all about the splendid apartments, the ceremonial, the princes and princesses, the great people, and all the other wonders I had seen!"

The success of Flandrin's paintings in the choir of Saint Germain des Prés was so great, that in December 1846 the Municipal Council asked him to undertake the proposed decoration of the Church of Saint Vincent de Paul, a work most attractive to Flandrin from an art point of view, as well as in respect of the two hundred thousand francs offered with the commission. But with his usual absolute unselfishness and consideration for others, Flandrin refused a commission he would gladly have accepted, out of delicacy towards his old master Ingres, who seems to have undertaken the work and then resigned it. It is not quite obvious wherein he could have been annoyed at Flandrin's acceptance of the task, for after his resignation, and before the offer was made to Flandrin, it had been offered to Paul Delaroche, who refused it. But anyhow, Flandrin feared to pain his beloved master, saying that "it would have been a grand and delightful undertaking, but my position with respect to M. Ingres is very delicate, and I would far rather give up the undertaking than run the slightest risk of wounding him. . . . . As I cannot accept the work, it has been intrusted to M. Picot, a member of the Institut, but the Prefect, in reply to the remonstrances of the Council, has promised that Saint Germain shall be finished, and, to say the truth, I think I should like that even better than the work I have refused."

As it happened, though Flandrin at last executed both these works, that of Saint Vincent de Paul was first taken in hand; for just as Picot was about to begin in 1848 the Revolution disturbed everything, and when a new town administration came into office, Armand Marrast, the Mayor, withdrew the commission to paint the Church of Saint Vincent from Picot and offered it to Flandrin. Disgusted at what he considered unfair treatment of a brother artist, Flandrin declined the task a second time, and it was only on Picot's own urgent representations that he would listen to any propositions on the subject, and even then he insisted on Picot taking part in the work as well as himself. Meanwhile, Flandrin worked on at Saint Germain des Prés. In a letter to his brother Paul, dated June 12, 1847, and referring to this

Church, he says: . . . . "I am quite worried by an idea which came into my head yesterday. Remembering that there is no really old tradition as to the colour of the Apostles' garments, I thought I would make them all white. You know one day you said something about it, so all night long I thought or dreamed about it. These twelve men uniformly white would be much more imposing, and have a finer effect than broken up into different tones, and moreover they are in Heaven, around the Throne of the Lamb. Morally it is far finer, but would the eye be as well satisfied as the mind? Would the whites harmonise with the whole tone of the decorations? That is what I wanted to try and find out to-day, by painting in Saint Matthew white, whom you saw violet. Unluckily it was not quite dry, and the under tints transpired somewhat, and consequently the white is not brilliant enough to enable me to judge definitely as to the effect. . . . . *June* 18*th.*—I consulted M. Ingres and M. Gatteaux, and both answered, 'Don't do it.' But notwithstanding, after a night of indecision, I decided on the white, and have now repainted three figures. MM. Ingres and Gatteaux came to Saint Germain, and both exclaimed, 'Bravo! it is really much better so!' entirely approving my determination; so now my mind is at rest, and I am getting on."

Another considerable work was about to devolve upon Flandrin, the decoration of the Church of St. Paul at Nîmes, in which he was assisted by his brother Paul, Louis Lamothe, already mentioned, and Paul Balze. In the autumn of 1847 the two Flandrins went to Nîmes, to study the ground on which they were to work, and to overlook the needful preparations. "We are in a little hotel, where some good people take ample care of us, but I have been terribly disappointed on going to see the Church and the preparatory works, which are very far from what they ought to be. The scaffolding is miserable, and must be put up afresh, and the walls are badly prepared. It is all very annoying." A year later, after a short visit to Lyons with wife and children (there was a second babe now), Flandrin took up his quarters at Nîmes, where the clear blue sky of the South recalled his beloved Rome; yet he was not generally attracted by the place, and seemed to feel the time of his abode there long. The Revolution disturbed Nîmes, always politically restless, and Flandrin was prepared for possible serious interruptions; but after some "red and socialist banquets," which produced a little surface commotion, the town returned to its ordinary aspect, and was quiet enough. Flandrin writes eagerly to Ambroise Thomas for intelligence as to the new constitution and the general attitude of Paris, saying that he and his fellow-labourers, engrossed from morning till night in their work, and hidden in the church which was the scene of that work, saw nobody, and had no means of knowing what was going on in the world they had left. For more than a month, Hippolyte says, they had not even received a letter able to put them at all up to the actual state of things, or the real tone of Paris.

"In spite of the delight of a work we rejoice in," Flandrin writes (Dec. 15, 1848) to his friend Victor Baltard, "we are keenly alive to our isolation and the separation from our friends. I can hardly believe that it is only two months since we left Paris. The time, as a whole, seems horribly long, although weeks go by like days, and days like hours. In order to get back as soon as possible to you all, I use them to the best of my power. Although the most splendid weather tempted us, and we should have liked to go and enjoy the glorious light and its effects on the rocks and the fair vegetation of the South, we resisted heroically. We have steadily given all working days up to work, so that we are really taking shape, and I am somewhat surprised myself to see how much we have been able to do in six weeks. . . . . The 10th passed off quietly here. There was plenty of life and animation, but the most perfect order everywhere. Louis Napoleon had 7000 votes; Ledru-Rollin from

1500 to 1600; Cavaignac from 1200 to 1300. Only it is said that Ledru-Rollin has a majority in the rest of the Department, and an immense number of votes all through the South, but I hope that the Centre and the North will restore things somewhat, and bring about a better result. Meanwhile I say, *Vive la Constitution!* and submit with the most absolute good faith to whatever universal suffrage may bring to pass, —it is the only possible basis in the present times for a political structure. And then I say with you, May God protect France! and I hope on. . . . . I have just received a letter from M. Hittorf about Saint Vincent de Paul, in which he says, among other things, that Varcollier professes to be greatly dissatisfied with me because of my coming to Nîmes and my work here. I must confess that this astonishes me, and I can only say that I am very sorry, for I know how friendly he has been to me in all this business. But what brought me here? I am fulfilling a promise, and that is what I hope all through life to do always. Moreover, I do not understand quite how any one can complain of my inactivity, inasmuch as in three months I have produced all the sketches and twenty-four metres of cartoons for the town. Anyhow, be so kind as to make my respects to M. Varcollier, and tell him that I am working so as to return to Paris by the beginning of the season, and that I am adding a third cartoon to two already done, which are about to be transferred to the wall."

"NÎMES, *Jan.* 5, 1849.

" . . . . Our *régime* here is much the same. We shut ourselves up within the four walls as soon as it is light, and do not come out again till dark. The days are too short, and we work by lamplight. We suffer from cold and rheumatism, albeit in the South, and I hope we shall have done by Easter. I can tell you it will have been by pulling hard against the collar."

It was during this pressure of work that Flandrin had a bad fall from one of his scaffolds, in which he was considerably hurt, but he did not give way to pain for an hour more than he could help, and in a few days, while yet stiff with bruises, he was again hard at work.

Flandrin alludes in one of the above-quoted letters to the "working days," and remembering how little such observation is general in France, especially perhaps, among men of his profession, it is interesting to find that he observed the rest of the Sunday. In a letter to his old master, M. Ingres, he says that their work "has had no interruption save that of Sundays. I long to submit this enormous work to you," he goes on to say, "and to hear your criticisms. I shall have to leave it so hastily that I shall hardly be able to take in the *ensemble*, or to keep a lasting impression of it. In order to judge of it and of myself somewhat fairly, I should like to see it again at the end of six months. My good helpers have been most devoted, and I think we have executed the paintings as rapidly as was possible. . . . . We have had a most enchanting climate during this winter, and the rare expeditions we could indulge in were so attractive that Paul thinks of staying on in this country to draw."

April found Flandrin still at Nîmes in spite of his uninterruptedly laborious toil. "It is so difficult to finish a work," he writes to Victor Baltard, "and this, which is one of the finest I could have to execute, has led me on further than I expected. I wish you could see it; I think you would say I was right to have sacrificed and braved a good deal in order to finish it. Besides, a host of bothers which one could not foresee have hindered me, and, in spite of a beautiful winter, we have worked as much as a fortnight together by lamplight. However, now I am really finishing, but I am so weary with this persistent work that I really must have a few days of rest."

Flandrin had reason to be satisfied with his work at Nîmes, which seems prodigious to have been accomplished within the time. In the apse he has painted a colossal Christ in Majesty, Saints Peter and Paul beside Him, and at His Feet a king and a slave, laying the one his crown, the other his chains, on the steps of the Throne; on the choir walls are three series of figures, representing the Evangelists, Archangels, and the Doctors of the Greek and Latin Churches; besides two processions of Martyrs and Virgins, a Coronation of the Blessed Virgin, and the Vision of S. Paul. Nor were these figures painted hastily, however rapid their production may have been. They were both conceived and executed in a spirit of deep devotion; as the Bishop of Nîmes, Monseigneur Plantier said, "Flandrin sought to preach after his own manner, and to him painting became eloquence, wherewith he uttered a magnificent profession of faith in the walls of God's Temples."

Bishop Plantier seems to have been intimate with Flandrin, and to have thoroughly appreciated the artist's deep and real religion, which as he says, had inspired him "with a conscientious love of art, so that painting was no mere profession in Flandrin's eyes, but a ministry, for the functions of which he prepared himself as an evangelist going forth to teach. Long since I remember discussing his future works with him, when he had been asked to decorate the Cathedral at Strasbourg, and the thing which struck me most was the religious awe with which he contemplated his task, and the earnest solicitude with which he collected the materials necessary to guide him. The bare idea of any voluntary shortcoming or negligence revolted not merely his artistic feelings, but his faith as a Christian. I shall never forget his saying to me in the most touching manner, 'Providence has constrained me to give myself up rather exclusively to religious art.' It was true. God, Who had claimed Overbeck's talents for Himself in Germany, seems in like manner to have claimed Flandrin in France, in order to prove to the nineteenth century, amid the reign of rationalism, that sincere faith and fervent love for the Church are not incompatible with the highest inspirations of art. . . . Heart and intellect combined in him to direct his talent. Too often amongst ourselves the Christianity of art is a mere circumstance, it renders a scene from the Gospel as it would one from Homer—its inspirations are factitious and shallow; but in Hippolyte the artist and Christian were absolutely one soul, his compositions and his moral graces sprung from a common source. He himself revered and worshipped that which he invited others to adore, and the saints who became the heroes of his pencil were also the models of his life. . . . He was just as simple in the practice of his religion as in the expression of his faith, and the combination of simplicity and superiority were very striking in him. If, to use a proverbial expression, he possessed *la foi du charbonnier*, he was no less possessed by the highest faith of genius, . . . and with all its vigour he combined its most refined delicacy. . . . Look at the procession of virgins in our Church of Saint Paul; every stroke, their attitude, the calm purity of glance, the seraphic expression of countenance, the grand severity of drapery, all tell of souls so pure that all about them is spiritualised, so that merely the indispensable material existence remains. And these pure forms are a correct indication of him who traced them—he too was transparent and clear as crystal."

As a whole, those best able to judge have pronounced Flandrin's frescoes at Nîmes as second to those in Saint Vincent de Paul in Paris. Perhaps the involuntary preference which he had for the one place over the other may have told upon his powers, and he continually missed the sympathy and counsel which he liked to seek from friends, and which could not be attained in the Southern city as in Paris. The latter part of the time spent at Nîmes was saddened by the death of several friends, as also by a severe illness which the precious little Auguste underwent; and up to the moment of departure Hippolyte was longing to be gone. When, however, the time really came, his affectionate heart had found roots, as it was wont to do everywhere, and he writes to his brother Paul, who lingered behind:—

"LYONS, *May* 11, 1849.

"I was grieved to leave you, and I felt leaving Nîmes and all our kind friends there very much. We had magnificent effects on sky and mountains, such poetical sights and significations! I think, my dear half (not shadow[1]), you ought to turn your attention specially to this side of art. Auguste was silent, except when now and then a duck crossing the road drew forth a shout of delight! Zizi was very good. We saluted the Pont du Gard from afar. . . . We took the boat at four o'clock (at Valence), but it did not get on, and when we made that remark to the captain he said quietly, 'Oh no, it's true she does not go so fast as the rest, but she can keep on at it longer!' So it ended in our reaching mama about ten o'clock. She looks well, and is not in the least altered. . . . If you notice anything you don't like in Saint Paul's, I leave it all to you; do whatever you think right." And a few days later he says, "Thank you for having touched up our pictures. You will go and see them again as you pass through Nîmes, won't you, and tell me what impression they leave on you? On the last day I was not at all satisfied, and I cannot shake off the recollection."

[1] This was in allusion to Paul Flandrin's habit of modestly calling himself his brother Hippolyte's "*ombre portée.*"

Flandrin reached Lyons quite ill from the effects of overwork and exhaustion, and the doctor insisted on his resting quietly there for a time. Quiet, however, was not to be had at command. It was the election time, and there was a serious popular outbreak. Flandrin describes it as follows:—

"LYONS, *June* 17, 1849.

"The day before yesterday Lyons was in great excitement, every one expecting news from Paris, and in spite of torrents of rain people gathered in groups all about the town. According to the Red newspapers, Ledru-Rollin was master of Paris, the President and ministers at Vincennes. Then the crowd swarmed over the Terreaux, and the quays, singing and announcing 'good news' for the next day. Although the rain never stopped, a host of people stayed all night in front of the Hôtel de Ville, shouting and hallooing. Some two hundred were arrested. Yesterday morning (Friday) I ran over to the Terreaux to fetch René, Mariette being ill. The place was crowded, and the Hôtel de Ville full of troops; only what is their mind? . . . The struggle was not believed to be so near, although we heard of sentinels disarmed, and soon we heard *feux de peloton*, and then guns from the Croix Rousse. I hurried off to fetch mama, who was with Mariette, and brought her home in great alarm. From eleven to three the guns in the Croix Rousse thundered incessantly against the barricades, then there came a pause of about three quarters of an hour. We heard nothing, the soldiers were in possession of the barricades, the bridges occupied by guns, and all communication between the two sides of the river suspended. All of a sudden the fusillade began again, extended down the quays, and came so near to us that a woman was wounded in her own house, Rue des Bouchers, No. 18. [It was No. 11 that the Flandrins inhabited.] Just then a ball struck our house as I was double-locking the outer gate. The firing went on till about half-past eight, and then gradually died away. It had hardly stopped when lightning and thunder began, and it seemed as though God's Voice were denouncing the horrors of the day. But, alas! this people seems deaf to all lessons! The day before all sorts of false intelligence was made up and circulated in order to bring about strife—the people know that. Again during the fighting the leaders set about other reports just as false, and they know that too. Yet nothing will open their eyes, and they go on with the same stupid idiotic faith in their deceivers. *Aux armes!* that is for ever their first and only cry, as if our institutions and liberties did not supply any other means of expressing our wants! The truth is, these gentlemen want to subject others and not to be subject themselves.

"General Gémeau, who commanded operations, acted with admirable decision. Everything was foreseen, arranged, and executed as rapidly as possible. But for that the evil might have reached a most alarming extent, and the country owes a great deal to men who dare to compromise and sacrifice themselves for it thus. A subscription is being raised for the wounded soldiers and for the families of those who were killed. I have just made my contribution; surely it is but fair that we should show our gratitude to our defenders when other people are so ready to spend money in seducing and corrupting."

Madame Flandrin was, not unnaturally, greatly shaken by the terror of this time, when shells were flying about her house, and dead and wounded carried beneath her windows; and at eighty (as she then was) such an alarm brought on serious illness, so that, in spite of her wonderful vigour and energy, great fears were entertained for her life. However, the danger passed away, and the venerable mother lived to enjoy the unfailing affection and care of her sons until February 1858, when she died, at the age of eighty-nine. When able to leave his mother without anxiety, Flandrin, though still very far from well, and often suffering acutely from rheumatism, which his long hours of work, often spent in cramped positions and in cold damp localities, tended too much to confirm, went back to Paris, and begun his work in the Church of Saint Vincent de Paul. In September 1849 he speaks of being comparatively free from pain for a few days together as of an unwonted thing. Flandrin's paintings in this church are considered by many as his finest work. Certainly no one will dispute the exceeding beauty and dignity of many of the figures which form the long processions on either side the nave; on the one Apostles, martyrs, doctors, bishops, and confessors; on the other virgin martyrs, holy women, penitents, and saintly household groups,—"pictorial litanies," as they have been graphically called. Those who delight to visit Saint Vincent de Paul, and gaze upon that wondrous group of imaged saints, will be interested in a little anecdote connected with the broad terrace which they will remember at the top of the flight of steps leading up to the west door, and which is specially characteristic of the master whose hand has decorated it. One September evening he had taken his little son there with him after dinner, and standing on the top of the broad steps, "I gazed in wondering admiration at the sky, one side of which still was bright with the glowing tints of the setting sun, while on the other the moon's bright orb rose silently. Auguste tried to count the stars. I talked to him about our Father in Heaven, and the child knelt down upon the stones, and leaning against the door with folded hands, began to pray for all of us." The training of this boy may be indicated by this, as well as by his father's thanks, five years later, to M. Ingres, on the occasion of his giving Auguste a Homer in that original Greek which Flandrin himself had so often longed to command; as also by a few brief lines addressed to the boy himself on his first going to school :—

"*Oct.* 6, 1858.

"My dear Auguste,—My dearest child, whenever you feel unhappy or dispirited, or if you should unfortunately be tempted by any bad example, in order to gain courage or avoid wrongdoing, think of God, Who has been so good to you hitherto; of the Blessed Virgin, who watches over you; of your dear loving mother; and of your father, whose happiness depends on your good conduct and well-doing. In short, love us as we love you."

Meanwhile the frescoes in Saint Vincent de Paul were progressing. Flandrin announces M. Ingres' inspection of them, and his approval, with as much satisfaction and modesty as in his earliest student days; and a little later he reports a visit from M. Berger, then Préfet de la Seine, who, after great admiration, inquired how long Flandrin would be occupied in this work, and, hearing that two years more were probably necessary, answered that in that case he would be ready quite at the right time for Saint Germain des Prés, which was destined for him to decorate. Flandrin tells his good prospects, laughing about his own "*bonheur insolant,*" with a half hesitation to his brother Paul, whose success he would fain have seen equal to his own. He never seemed eager about acquiring honours or praise, though eager enough about the success of his work. Thus he neither expresses great disappointment at his failure on two occasions (in 1849 and 1851) to be elected a member of the Académie, nor great exultation when, in 1853, he became a successful candidate for this dignity.

In the autumn (1851) some rest became absolutely necessary, and Flandrin went to the South of France with his wife and children. He writes from Avignon to his brother: "I have just been to Notre Dame. From the high terrace in front of the church there was a most glorious view; the sun was just sinking, the Rhine and the plain in shadow, but the Ventaux and the chain of Alps lit up with its last bright rays. Glorious! glorious! and then that ancient church, with its grand images in front. It was open, and I went in and said a little prayer for you and for us."

Tidings of the death of the Flandrins' first master, Legendre Héral, reached him at Marseilles; and after some kindly and religious expression of feeling, and allusions to their education in art, Flandrin goes on to bid Paul "always strive to get at the poetical meaning of nature, to find the most beautiful and most true side of everything, inasmuch as that it is which is most closely bound to things eternal, which is, in short, the moral sense that unites man to God."

In 1852 Flandrin had the great delight of seeing his brother receive the Cross of the Legion of Honour, which, as he says, brightened up his own marvellously. A year later he himself received the higher dignity of "Officier de l'Ordre de la Légion d'Honneur," and in 1854 he was appointed to a Professorship in the École des Beaux Arts. His strength seems often to have failed amid the pressure of work, at home and abroad, for he painted a good many portraits during the time that his great frescoes were in hand, the demands upon his purse being considerable; and he says to his brother that his labour was as necessary as the first day he set to work, although he felt that he no longer could work as he had done, but that everything became a toil. His constant aim to preserve a quiet mind amid labour, anxiety, or popularity is very striking. "*Il ne faut pas se troubler*," he says, "if only I could practise that admirable precept." An occasional trip to the sea, Eu, Tréport, or Havre, revived him, and his keen appreciation of all natural beauty, sea, sky, sunset, or moonlight, generally brings back some remembrances of that artist's paradise, his beloved Rome. The work in Saint Vincent de Paul was finished at last, in 1854, and the following year Flandrin engaged in another considerable undertaking of the same kind at Lyons. Before going there to decorate the church of Ainay, he had to take part as one of the judges in that redoubtable Exhibition field wherein he had formerly suffered so much. His vivid recollection of his own early days made the office a painful one. He writes to his mother:—

"PARIS, *April* 1855.

"I have been stupid enough to be rather ill again. All the plaster was new in the Salles d'Exposition where we held our jury of decision, the rain and snow came in; in short, I caught cold, and was obliged to take to my bed. . . . All this jury business does not please me at all. One must reject people who believe in their own talent, and bestow maledictions on you for the vexations inflicted on them, just as they may be. Of course here and there one or two people there may be who are dealt with severely, and made to grieve unjustly, but it is almost impossible that it should be otherwise. Still it does not the less grieve your son, who you know does not like much better than his dear mother to see any one distressed, especially humble folk. Altogether I shall not be at all sorry when I can return to my own business."

In July of that year (1855) Flandrin took up his quarters at Lyons in order to paint the Church of Ainay. He found the Curé ready to trust him thoroughly, and the first measure taken was to get an order from that gentleman to have all his scaffolding taken down and put up anew, as it had been prepared so as to make painting impossible! There were other drawbacks when he began to paint; the walls were badly prepared, and so wet that the first outlines had to be drawn three times; then a platform on the scaffolding gave way, and Flandrin had a fall, not from any important height, but enough to sprain both his feet and cause him to lose several days. The church was dark, the lights inconvenient, and July though it was, several days were so gloomy, that he said a candle would have been acceptable! and the curves of the rounded parts of the building, which necessarily altered the outlines of his figures, were troublesome. Another trouble to which Flandrin was sensitive, was that every one in the church could see what was going on, and, as he says, criticism set to work as soon as there were four strokes drawn! Flandrin declared to his brother that if he had known all the difficulties beforehand which were to beset him, he would never have undertaken the work. "I am ruining my sight, and take what trouble I may, I believe this work will never count as worth much!" This however was an unnecessarily gloomy view of the matter, and there were many who, like the Bishop of Nîmes (whose opinion and criticism Flandrin invited), saw a grand poem written on the three apses (if it be correct so to call the terminal *absides* of the aisles) of Ainay Church. Behind the high Altar is a grand figure of Our Lord blessing the world, with the Blessed Virgin, Saints Blandina and Clotilde, the Archangel S. Michael, Saint Pothinus, the Apostle of Lyons, and S. Martin. In the smaller right hand apse is Saint Benedict seated in his Abbot's chair, with two monks at his feet dedicating the Abbey of Ainay to his Rule, and on the other side Saint Badulph.

The following year Flandrin returned to Saint Germain des Prés, where he was commissioned to paint the nave, that is the intervals between the windows, containing forty figures, and eighteen groups in the spaces between the arcades and windows. The former represent the principal types and promises of Holy Scripture from Adam and Eve to Zacharias, from Noah to Saint John Baptist, while the lower groups consist of prophecies from the Old and fulfilments from the New Testaments. Thus, Balaam prophesying the Star which should arise in Judah is beside the adoration of the Magi; Joseph sold by his brethren by the Betrayal; the Tower of Babel beside the Mission of Pentecost, and so on. If the writer may be permitted here to hazard an opinion as to the merits of Flandrin's paintings, one is tempted to say, that among these groups his finest works are to be found; the dignity, poetry, and devotional feeling of many of those groups are marvellous. Perhaps Flandrin himself enjoyed this more than any other of his works. He had completed the nave, and was occupied in preparing to paint the transept (or arm of the cross in which the church is built), when death closed his earthly labours in God's service. When he left Paris in 1864 Flandrin foresaw that he should not live to complete the work. "Le bon Dieu ne veut pas que je finisse sa maison," he said, with a touching smile of resignation, conscious of the weakness to which illness had reduced him.

Always reticent and free from the self-consciousness which leads us to dwell largely on our own doings, Flandrin writes but little of this his favourite work; the few times he alludes to it in his letters are very characteristic, as when he writes to his landscape painter brother Paul (while painting Adam and Eve in Paradise, and Moses before the burning bush), "I am working at life-size landscape myself, and as the best way out of my difficulty, I have a mind to go and see if your concierge will let me make one or two studies in your atelier;" and in another letter to M. Laurens, he says: "I am working at the nave of Saint Germain des Prés—just at this moment on the subject of God rebuking Adam and Eve after their fall; is it not enough to make one tremble?"

His failing health involved many absences and attempts at gaining strength. In September 1859 Hippolyte describes to Paul a journey just ended:—

"At Arles, we went to the Hôtel du Forum—pah! what filth! The town was sweltering under a sirocco, the very stones trickled, the sky lowered heavily, but all the same how I enjoyed re-visiting Saint Trophime and the Cloister, the Theatre and Arena. And all those beautiful and interesting things in the Musée! The head of Diana is a marvel, the Silenus, the Four dancers, the young Roman, are all worth hearty study, and though I saw them too hastily, they have left very delightful recollections behind. In spite of the railroad Arles is Arles yet; the women keep their beauty and their costume, and the Southern flavour is strong and entire. At Tarascon, Avignon, and Orange, through which we merely passed, I devoured regretfully everything with my eyes! Le Ventaux was cloud-capped. Then came Montélimart, Valence, Saint Vallier: the South is slipping from us, yet at

Vienne, and still more at Lyons, we found a sky which somewhat recalled it. We decided on sleeping at the Perrache station, and the next day, with pleasant though somewhat changeable weather, we went from Lyons to Paris. Less and less of the beloved South, but nature always affords food for admiration, causes for praising God and thanking Him. We came back to the Forest of Fontainebleau, etc., in the light of one of the finest sunsets I have ever been given to behold. Paris was quite dark, the *macadam* still wet with yesterday's rain. Here is our own dear street; we got out of the carriage, and you can fancy our delight in hearing our poor little Paul[1] shouting our names with all his might. Next day I had to see to a heap of letters and papers. I hurried off to the École to see the pictures in competition. . . . My day was so full I could not write sooner."

"BLOIS, *Aug*. 31, 1860.

"My dear Paul,—It has rained, it does rain, it will rain! You will remember we had three tolerable days; and so we packed up, but meanwhile the weather lowered, and when the cab came to take us to the railroad, there was no room for doubt; it rained hard enough to appal people who have not been case-hardened by the last eight months' *régime*. All the same we set

[1] Hippolyte Flandrin's third child.

out, took our tickets and places, and started. Through the rain we made out Étampes, the plains of La Beauce, Orléans, Beaugency, and at last Blois. Forty-four *lieues* through this torrent of rain and a driving wind. Then came a short respite. We went into an intensely picturesque town, guarded by its fine castle. After taking possession of rooms in the hôtel, we armed ourselves with umbrellas, and headed by Paul, we went all about that great monument, penetrated within, saw it from top to bottom, and admired inside and out alike. What a blessing that the restoration has been intrusted to M. Dauban, to whom we owe, not a mere preservation, but the very new birth of a *chef-d'œuvre* of originality and beauty. What poor wretched artists we are in comparison to such as those! On leaving the Château, we climbed to the heights in order to see the Loire, but the wind was violent, the clouds heavy and low, and we were soon driven back to the picturesque old streets, full of interesting old houses. We went to the churches, and at last came in to rest and dine—raining still. In the evening we went with umbrellas to the fair on the Quays. When we went to bed the clouds were dispersing, and the moon bright, but this morning the rain is coming down steadily again, with a pretence of innocent good faith which is most irritating; it looks as if it would never leave off! Nevertheless we have ordered a carriage to go and see Chambord, four *lieues* distant. . . . ."

Some idea of the way in which work was crowded upon Flandrin,—the successful artist as he had become, —may be gathered from a letter to M. Lacuria, dated

"PARIS, *Jan.* 25, 1861.

" . . . . My life becomes more and more harassing. In addition to the old tasks which more than filled it, I am now *à la mode!* As I told you before, the success—absurd, because it was beyond bounds—of two poor portraits[1] has brought about this glut of applications. I have refused at least one hundred and fifty since the last Exhibition, but there are certain princes, ministers, etc., who demand, or command, with a persistence which drives me to despair, and to whom I submit with so bad a grace, that I am visibly dwindling away. *C'est fini*, I have ceased to be a painter! Farewell to study, and to that delightful hope of improvement which kindles all one's vigour and strength. This sort of good fortune crushes me, and I wish I knew how to get free from it, of which I have no hope! And yet, if even that were all! . . ."

[1] One of these was a portrait of Mademoiselle Maison, now Madame la Baronne de Mackau, which, on being exhibited in 1859, at once obtained the name of "*la jeune fille à l'œillet.*"

Repeated failures of health, over-work, and a journey to Allevard les Bains, seem to have been the history of that year. Flandrin writes, August 15th, to his brother Paul, who, by the way, was married before this:—" . . . . Monday was the hottest day I ever knew in Paris; when our packing was done we were exhausted, and I felt it was very imprudent to start in such a torrid heat. . . . . However, we set off at seven in the evening, and were fortunate enough to have our compartment to ourselves, and whenever any one was likely to get in, we all six poked our heads out so as to keep off intruders. In about two hours' time we said our prayers as though at home, and little Paul slept till four o'clock, when the sun roused him up. Near Châlons the sky brightened, the stars vanished, and soon the Saône glittered amid the sweet plains round Maçon. . . . . We came to the beautiful valley you remember so well. . . . . All my dear old childish memories seized upon me. At Culoz we took the Victor Emanuel line, crossing the Rhône, coasting the Lac de Bourget, and stopping at Aix and Chambéry. At Montmélian we left the railroad. It was eleven o'clock, horribly hot, and very tiring; we were broiled and stifled, as you and I were sometimes of old in Italy."

Flandrin rejoiced in the beauty of the scenery around, and would fain have indulged in his brother's department of landscape painting, but his eyes were suffering, and he had to give them rest. He had hoped to go on to his "dear South," but the *Concours de Rome* was coming on, and he felt bound to assist at it. Stopping at Lyons on their way back to Paris, Flandrin wrote that the pleasure he had expected to find in returning there was destroyed by his bad health. "These three days I have been unable to see either people or things. The first evening of our arrival I went at nine o'clock with Auguste and Cécile, and gazed at our dearest mother's windows, and as I was speaking with emotion of her dear memory, I felt a tear fall on my hand, and Cécile was crying quietly. These tears of my children were very soothing to me I must confess."

Among the portraits Flandrin was called upon to paint in his heyday of popularity was that of the Emperor Napoleon III. (exhibited 1863, and afterwards placed in the Luxembourg). He alludes to it in a letter to M. Laurens, dated

"PARIS, *Dec.* 10, 1861.

"I have been long answering you, but I have been under tremendous fire—finishing my paintings in Saint Germain, or rather preparing to uncover what is finished, for there is a lot still to compose and execute. About a fortnight since the scaffolding was removed, and I saw the *ensemble* for the first time.

Then I went to spend a week at Compiègne. Can you fancy me in shorts, with a crush hat under my arm? Indeed, dear friend, I was not at my ease! Nevertheless, their Majesties, really courteous, treated their guests most kindly, and took pains to provide for their pleasure. We had *chasse à tir*, *à course*, and *curée*—balls, plays, etc., but all that is not worth the good daily bread of work, and one's own free studio and fireside! Still this visit will not have been unprofitable with a view to my portrait of the Emperor, and I know my sitter much better now than before."

The run upon Flandrin's portraits continued. He writes to M. Lacuria from Auteuil:—

"*June* 29, 1862.—I am not delivered from portrait-painting, but I am a little less beset, and I profit by it to return to that which ought to engross me entirely, and which, between ourselves, is much less wearisome to me. . . . . Health permitting, we are making an attempt to get to Rome, after which I have been sighing these twenty-four years, and the sight of which I fancy would do me a world of good morally. I was imprudent enough to talk of going there before the children, who are wild to go; and if anything obliges us to defer the journey till another year there will assuredly be great lamentations. As to myself, I feel that I have already postponed it too long, and that if I could have indulged in such enjoyment some years ago it would have greatly added to my powers in the work at Saint Germain des Prés. Well, we think, and long to go, but all the while we know that a thousand things may hinder us.

"How I should enjoy going over the Campana collection with you, that new source of material for the study of art from the very earliest time to our own day! This altogether unique collection ought to be most carefully preserved apart from our other treasures. Unfortunately the *Administration des Musées* is intent on doing everything in its power to absorb it and swell the collections of the Louvre, which ought only to be added to by an occasional *chef-d'œuvre,* while everything of inferior merit is weeded out. The Emperor has heard everything that can be said on this behalf already; but perhaps he will yield from want of localities to contain the treasures, or money to create fresh ones.

"You have doubtless heard of M. Ingres' nomination to the dignity of Senator. It is a graceful homage on the part of the authorities, for which I feel very grateful to the Emperor, with whom it originated. When M. Ingres went to thank the Minister, M. Walewski, he replied, 'I rejoice in your nomination with all my heart, but it is entirely the Emperor's own doing.' Moreover, the fact was announced in a charming letter to Madame Ingres from the Empress, who wished to be the first with her congratulations, expressed most graciously and nobly. There is a general satisfaction felt at this act of justice towards the chief of our French school of art, and only here and there some slight growling. We felt that this was an occasion for expressing to our master all the gratitude and respect we feel for him, his example and his teaching; so some forty of his pupils and old Roman students met at my house, and we voted an address to him, and a gold medal with his likeness, and the inscription 'A Jean-Auguste Dominique Ingres, Peintre d'histoire, Sénateur, ses élèves et ses admirateurs.' The address is at the École des Beaux Arts, where all who will are signing it. I know your mind so well that I was sure you would approve of my signing it for you. . . . I agree with you, in order to progress, one must recollect one's-self and obey the dictate of one's heart; I believe it is the only way to reach other men's hearts. Simplicity and sincerity are our greatest strength. I must watch; I sometimes feel that too constant work in one groove tends to a falling off."

Flandrin had been for some time on the Commission des Beaux Arts of the Préfecture de la Seine, and he was also on a Commission lately established by M. Walewski, which, among other duties, was expected to advise the Minister concerning commissions, purchases, and rewards to be given to artists.

The journey to Rome did not take place that autumn. Flandrin writes to his brother from Paris, Aug. 2, 1862: "Never, no, never have I been so tormented, distracted, and hustled as I was lately. Distribution of works for the town and Ministère, the Emperor's fête, when all the nominations for the Legion of Honour are made, elections at the Institut, at the École des Beaux Arts, and everywhere else! It is enough to drive one wild! I am becoming simply idiotic, and the only thing which surprises me is that I have any energy left to try to work! but, as you may imagine, all this pleasant engrossment of my time, with an almost entirely failing sight, produces a woful result. . . . Without wishing to murmur against the events which keep us apart, dear Paul, I do grieve over it. What a blessing it would be if we could spend a summer together, meeting to talk over everything as in old times, under some kindly tree! Unfortunately it does not seem as though rest were meant to be had in this world. So we must make ready for it in the next by leading good lives, and patiently accepting the troubles and vexations which abound here."

An interesting letter to M. Lacuria gives Flandrin's impression of some of the great works of art in Belgium :

"*October* 19, 1862.— . . . We went first to Lille to see the magnificent collection of Raffaele's and Michael Angelo's drawings in the Musée there. Raffaele shines in quantity and quality of his incomparable works—it is a real treasure. Thence we went to Bruges, a striking town in the character of its private dwellings, as well as in churches, markets, Hôtel de Ville, etc. Above all, there is a public Palace, which to my eyes is a very type of such buildings belonging to the rich and powerful communities of the fourteenth century. The Hôpital Saint Jean contains many deservedly famous and precious paintings of Hemling. The churches, which are fine and remarkable, have all acquired a something peculiar since the Spanish dominion, which strikes one a good deal. Those beautiful large Gothic naves are often cut in two by jubes [roodlofts or galleries] in black and white marble, and overladen with ornaments, pictures, sculptures, wood carvings. There are some very beautiful things among these, which we looked at again and again with the most intense interest, but unfortunately I had not time to draw.

"We were very much struck by our visit to the Béguinage—here in some forty humble houses (but so clean as to defy all description!) a number of women live in retreat, bound by no vows, but under one rule, and wearing a fixed dress. The houses surround an irregular square of soft turf, shadowed by fine trees. The peace and calm of the place are infectious, and one feels as if an asylum there from time to time would be a great boon. The whole town is curious and interesting, and its early painters have supplied me with memories by which I would fain profit. What wonderful men the brothers Van Eyck were!

"From Bruges we went to Ghent, which as a town rather disappointed me; the modern element has so greatly effaced its old aspect. Still it is rich in many ways, but the one attraction to me is in the Cathedral of Saint Bavon,—Jan Van Eyck's Triumph of the Lamb. The whole arrangement of the subject, the light and colour blend into perfect poetry, the effect of which is increased as you penetrate farther, and study the character and moral sense of all the figures. I don't think I ever saw such a combination of beauty. We went back to this picture three times in one day. The churches in Antwerp are full of Rubens' and Van Dyck's; some of the Rubens' are certainly much finer than any that we possess. They are magnificent, and so finished, that while looking at them one asks no more; but turn to the early pictures, and they make one forget all this magnificent and splendid talent, for they appeal directly to one's heart, and leave lasting impressions there. There is much more to tell, but time fails. I must only say that we went on to Brussels, Malines (a charming town), Louvain, Liège, Aix la Chapelle, and lastly Cologne, taking Namur on our return. There are many beautiful and touching objects of interest at Cologne, in the cathedral and in the many ancient churches, which are ossuaries for thousands of martyrs. Only we found it very difficult to communicate with the inhabitants, and ought to be highly proficient by this time in the art of pantomime, in spite of which we often were forced to give up all hope of understanding or being understood. At last we returned to Paris, which seemed horrid; indeed, I don't know any place where the houses are so ugly and without form. The Rue de l'Abbaye, which I care for most of all, received us quietly, and we heartily thanked our good God for having given the five of us this enjoyable outing, with fine weather and no ill-health."

This last year did not diminish Flandrin's occupation or responsibilities. "Days, months, fly by," he writes (St. John's Day, 1863), "and soon a year, which has been all but lost as far as work is concerned, will be gone. My two last compositions for the nave of Saint Germain des Prés are not yet finished, and yet I do most earnestly desire to go to work at them again." One very engrossing duty was the *Jury des récompenses*, to which Flandrin always devoted his full hearty attention, at whatever cost to his own immediate pursuits. He was not altogether satisfied with this year's Exhibition. "We get little else now," he says (June 1863), writing to M. Lacuria, "but *peinture de genre.* Among that class of works we find charming things, a great deal of talent and feeling, and certain landscapes in colouring and style put forth one side of truth, which is not without its value, but which to my mind is only secondary. Form is a point more and more neglected, and yet physiognomy, character, the moral sense of things, are strictly in its domain. Is not everything grand in art dependent on good drawing? I may be mistaken, but it seems to me that photography has inflicted a mortal blow on art. Many people, with its aid, and industry, can perform things otherwise left undone, but where shall we find that vigorous drawing, that living spirit which we admire in great masters, and which can only be the result of constant observation and study of nature?

"You will have heard of the Venuses, by Cabanel and Baudry! Both works are remarkable for different qualities; only why do not such clever men put themselves under the banner of ancient art? They would acquire more power to avoid seeking those endless refinements and insipid prettinesses which may win present success, but which, perhaps, may not keep it long."

About the same time Flandrin mentions that he had just received the Prussian Order of Merit, with a letter from the artist Cornelius, which he says makes him feel quite ashamed, from the thought that so many honours have been showered upon him as compared to many of his brethren in art, whose greater merits are so little recognised. Characteristically enough, his first idea seems to be the satisfaction his old master would derive from this compliment, and the news was taken to M. Ingres as an offering certain to be acceptable for his fête-day.

Illness pressed more and more heavily on the painter; he felt less and less able to encounter the endless worries and anxieties which his position, public and private, involved; and in the autumn of 1863 he resolved to leave all behind and carry out the long-cherished plan of a winter in Italy, where he hoped to recruit his failing bodily strength, and to get some degree of mental rest and refreshment; determined, as he said, "to do nothing but do homage to my beloved Rome." He grieved to leave his work at Saint Germain des Prés unfinished, but though saying that "God would not have him finish His House," Flandrin looked hopefully at that time to restored health and renewed energy at his work. But in fact he left Paris, on October 18, 1863, never to return. In his Journal he dwells upon the beautiful but somewhat melancholy aspect of the country in its autumnal hues, adding that, as the train whirled on, memories of early days at Lyons and at Rome rose up vividly in his mind, and he had been going far back into the first phase of his life. The travellers, consisting of Flandrin, his wife and three children, and M. Laurens, paused at Lyons, and there his last act in his native land was to go "*là haut*," as he always described the cemetery where his father and mother were buried, and pray beside their graves. Friendly hands had decorated their graves with fresh flowers, and Flandrin was deeply touched at the little incident. There had been many changes and chances since the days when the "petits Flandrin" used to pick up stray lessons from M. Duclaux how to draw animals, with a view to their intended line as painters of battle-pieces. M. Duclaux was still living at Lyons, and Flandrin tried to see him, as well as the few relations still dwelling there, but he was absent. They left Lyons, on October 20th, for Marseilles, proceeding again thence by railway to Nice. Flandrin's admiration of the scenery is ecstatic. "The variety, the richness of outline, of form and effect, altogether exhausted my powers of expression—I could only hold up my hands! Indeed, the journey to Nice is more wondrous than I can possibly say. If I were a landscape-painter, I think I should feed upon this country for long.

"On the 24th we left Nice by a fine road which winds among the mountains, and after two hours and a half ascent, we reached the summit, and saw the sea again, as also the Alps and their glaciers; the Gulf of Villafranca, and its guest the Montebello, at our feet. For a long time we kept on the heights, and saw Eza lying beneath us, a little nest of Saracen pirates, perched on an isolated rock. Now the Saracens are replaced by Christians, and the little church rises gracefully amid the poor village which stands in a cleft of the rock. By degrees we descended—road superb,—passed Turbia, an ancient Roman station, . . . Monaco, bright and smiling, in the bottom, and a little further on, Roccabrucca and Mentone, our last possession on the Italian side. We reached our hôtel at four o'clock, and went out directly to go close to the sea, to wet our feet in it as the waves advanced; and then we went all over the little town, climbing from street to street, from terrace to terrace, up to the three churches which, grouped together, crown it. The cathedral is large and grand after a fashion, but what taste in general! Painting is downright abused, for you see houses of every colour, yellow, white, pink, green. Just opposite our hôtel[1] is

[1] Flandrin must have stayed at the Hôtel de Londres.

the Hôtel de Turin, which is painted ultramarine, with green shutters, and turned up with yellow. Beyond the frontier, *in Italia* proper, nothing is more common than blue houses, pink turrets, striped façades; yet all the while this brilliant architecture, which is not often good, presents delicious bits of outline and proportion. All the little towns have a character of their own, and a special grace. At Mentone I was struck with the beauty of some of the women and children, especially with their gentle, good expression. On Sunday morning we went to Mass, and then started again with our vetturino. A little further we came to Ventimiglia, a pretty little fortified town, crossing the road. There we breakfasted at La Locanda d'Italia, and I tried my Italian for the first time. We breakfasted opposite a sort of chapel to the *Re galant' uomo* and Garibaldi. From Bordighera to San Remo—shore covered with a real wood of palm trees. The streets and *ensemble* of San Remo are very striking, lofty palaces adorned with porticos, *loggia*, terraces, reminding one of Spanish towns. Being Sunday, the people were all out; we saw lovely women, and I regret most heartily not having been able to preserve any of those beautiful types. So again at Porto Maurizio and Oneglia. If I could but draw instead of writing!

"*October 26th.*—Off at seven o'clock. Sea calm,

dolphins playing on the surface, as though saluting the rising sun. By degrees the mountains grow lower, and there are more villages amid the boundless forest of olive trees which shrouds them like a soft curtain. At Loano (where Massena fought the Austrians and Sardinians) we breakfasted. A large lady, with a huge crinoline, assisted by her daughter and a cameriera in crinolines to match, showed us into the salon, which was neither more nor less than a shrine to Garibaldi. . . . . Thence to the salle-à-manger, where we had a rustic but tolerable meal; that was all very well, but what was not so well was the ridiculously exorbitant bill."

"*October 27th.*—Left Savona at eight o'clock. Weather and country both beautiful. But the olive trees are becoming fewer and smaller—one only sees a palm tree here and there, and the caroubas are replaced by ilex. As we approached Genoa (seeing its beautiful clusters and striking *faro* from a great distance) the houses became more red, more green, more blue, and above all more yellow, and were decorated with the most fantastic architectural inventions, the most comical ornamentation. My little Paul unconsciously made a happy criticism, exclaiming, 'Oh, papa, look at all these card-houses!' On reaching the Lanterne, at the entry of the port, we saw the whole of Genoa, and I can well understand her being called the Superb. The height of her houses and palaces, the profusion of her towers, domes and belfries, her bold groups of buildings, give to the whole a proud look of wealth very suitable to the reputation of this rival to Venice."

They lionized Genoa, much as everybody does, and started again for Sestri on the 29th, breakfasting at the little solitary inn on the heights midway, so familiar—with its glorious view and vine-covered trellises—to all Mediterranean travellers. Flandrin's enjoyment of the scenery was intense, and his description of the colouring of the Pass of Bracco will bring the scene vividly to many a memory. "Olive trees are replaced by ilex, and then by chesnuts, and at last the huge mountain sides are clothed by a scanty dun fleece—often bare. Above Bracco, at the top of the ascent, which took three hours, we found bare ground of every colour, from black and violet to sulphur tints, separating us from the dark rocks which hid their summits amid the clouds—a very embodiment of chaos and desolation. No trace of man beyond the road, except when from one of the steepest points a young girl came running down through the fog to see us pass, and then stood motionless, gazing and smiling—a lovely picture contrasting with the wild landscape."

At Borghetto (where, as elsewhere, they encountered a perpetual glorification of Garibaldi) they were stopped by the old grievance—floods on the Magra. An English family and the Princess Orloff shared the Flandrins' detention of two days, one of which was All Saints' Day, when the somewhat rude but hearty services of the little village church touched the painter with a great sense of reality and simplicity. From Sarzana to Pisa he was again in raptures over the scenery, which, he says, should make the fortune of a landscape-painter. Pisa was an old friend, and renewed his former impressions, "with its tranquil streets, vast palaces and lovely churches, around which the grass grows freely." He took his wife and children to see the town. "The four great monuments appeared at once all golden against a glorious blue sky. The Leaning Tower is as disagreeable to me as before. I don't like that sort of curiosity. After dwelling upon the external view of this rare combination of buildings, we went to the Baptistry, where the interior architecture especially struck us with its grandeur and boldness, and withal its simplicity.

"The Campo Santo, which I remembered as one of the things which had struck me most, fully confirmed my former impressions; the simplicity of its architecture, where severity and elegance are so blended, struck me fully as much as in my youth. It was with real emotion that I entered and saw the ravages time has made on those venerable walls. Some treasures are altogether departed, and the rest are fading fast. Orcagna's grand subjects are treated with a power and pathos such as they deserve, but the life of San Ranieri is much damaged, and Benozzo Gozzoli's great work is fading. Some frescoes are still tolerably perfect, some groups worthy of Masaccio, which I would fain see preserved."

Flandrin and his eldest boy went over to Lucca, and he was greatly impressed by the cathedral, with its exquisitely rich sculptured porch, and with the two famous Fra Bartolommeos in San Romano. He took a regretful farewell of the Campo Santo before leaving Pisa. "The last rays of the setting sun still lingered upon it, but soon they passed away, and we had sorrowfully to say goodbye. Then we went into the cathedral, where nothing could be distinguished save the great masses, still more imposing in the shadow and stillness. That too we had to leave. Alas, it is passing too rapidly over such glorious things!"

They next went to Sienna, which greatly delighted Flandrin. He thought the Piazza and the Palazzo almost the finest things he had seen. His admiration of Nicola Pisano was great. "What grand meaning this master gives to all he touches! I had him always in high reverence, but I must confess that this reverence increases with every fresh work of his that I see; they satisfy my mind entirely. . . . We all went together to see the Palazzo del Governo, built by Popes Pius II. and III., both Piccolomini, with the delicious *loggia* adjoining, which is, to my mind, one of the most important among the glories of Sienna, as is the Porta Romana. It is marvellous how the artists of that period knew how to give each building its individual meaning. This gate, according as it is open or shut, becomes a triumphal arch or an invincible defence. It faces the enemy with wondrous daring, yet not without a pious thought; for the little chapel suspended over the passage sets forth a representation of Him under Whose Protection the town reposes. From beneath the arch of this strong yet simple building we looked out upon an enchanting landscape lit up with the autumn sun. . . . Truly Sienna is the queen of towns."

Flandrin went to see M. Mussini, Director of the Sienna Academy, who showed him all the treasures it possesses of old masters, and at last they left Sienna, feeling that a much longer stay would have been enjoyable. Thence the travellers proceeded by Orvieto, Bolsena, Montefiascone and Viterbo, all full of memories of past times. Flandrin remembered saying thirty years ago to Paul, as they coasted the lake, that it was beautiful enough for the new creation fresh from God's Hand! Coming in sight of the dome of Saint Peter's, all the party got out of the carriage to do it homage, and as they entered the Piazza del Popolo Flandrin's delight and emotion grew overwhelming.

Once again in his beloved Rome; whither, indeed, he had come to die! But as yet it was all excitement and delight. Almost as soon as they had arrived he hastened to his old haunts, and after dining at Lepri's, "we instinctively took the Trinità de' Monti steps, and, following the Pincio, now dark and deserted, I hastened to show the front of the Villa Medici to my wife and children. Like a lover gazing upon his lady's windows, I gazed; I would fain have touched the walls within which I had been so happy; but there were people about the door, whom I supposed to be students, and after a moment's contemplation, we beat our retreat by the Salita and the Via San Sebastiano." Flandrin wrote enthusiastically of the same event to his brother: "There it was indeed —the dear dwelling—where I, where *we* were so happy! Hidden among the ilexes, I dipped my fingers in the fountain as if it were a bénitier, and gazed. . . . . I could almost reproach myself for coming here without you; our mutual love makes it almost painful to have any enjoyment apart. But as we cannot always be together, we must thank God for the pangs which prove how dearly we love one another."

The weather was rainy, but while his wife was occupied in settling into an apartment in the Piazza di Spagna, Flandrin could not resist taking his children to some of the most striking scenes in Rome;—St. Peter's, which he admired even more than of old, saying that "there is a majesty and supernatural power about it not to be found in kings' palaces;" the Forum and Coliseum, amid thunder and torrents of rain, whence he and Auguste returned dripping like fish; the Pantheon, Raffaele's tomb, the Loggia and Stanze. "The sight of these masterpieces, whose memory is as deep in my heart as my head, kindled all my enthusiasm; what intense delight to realise all this beauty! Oh, dear Paul, why are you not here?" And he assures M. Ingres that the "intensity of their poetry and beauty has given me new life."

Flandrin gave himself up to seeing Rome anew, and showing its wonders of delight to his wife and children. "It is inexhaustible," he writes. "How many things I had not seen, or seen imperfectly, which indeed I should doubtless see better now if I knew more. But, I can assure you, I go to work with a good will which is very enjoyable, and the delight of my belongings adds to mine. Every day we make some excursion, on foot or driving, and for the last four weeks the weather has been fine, the sun brilliant, almost scorching; but, on the other hand, in the shade it is so cold that I dare not lay aside my cloak. . . . Except these troubles (connected with the Academy), which give me sleepless nights, and so are weakening, I am very happy, and I don't know what I could do more likely to set me up again. I am at Rome,—well lodged, in full sunshine, the weather perfect, I am out all day enjoying the scenes I most delight in,—what conditions could be more favourable for recovering my health? Yet, unfortunately, to my great grief, I feel as enervate as ever, arms and legs broken! Anyhow nobody can say now that it is caused by over-work, for the last two months I have done absolutely nothing but eat, drink, and sleep, and enjoy the sunshine."

His Journal betokens the energy with which Flandrin revisited every point of interest—the Catacombs, churches innumerable, where his devout spirit and his artist's taste alike found rest; pictures, statues, excavations—all were a fresh source of delight to him. The Academia calls forth his enthusiasm: "Everything there is so beautiful that I overflow with delight and admiration, the palace more lovely than ever, the laurels greener—the plain, the mountains with their crown of fresh snow—the whole thing together makes me cry out aloud to myself! Then the *bosco*, still more beautiful; and feeling that I must tell it all to some one, I hurried home to make all my dear ones share my delight!" He dined in the old hall with the students, "and felt like a student again myself,—the reception given me, so hearty and affectionate, touched me deeply."

"ROME, *Dec.* 4, 1863.

"My dear Paul,— . . . I have been to the Stanze to-day, and, for the first time since my arrival, to the Museo, to the Transfiguration, the Coronation, the Madonna del Foligno, and revelled in them. I pastured in all their beauty, greater, fresher than ever. I would I could say the same of the frescoes! Alas, it appears to me that some of the Loggia have suffered, and that there are tokens of advancing ruin in the Stanze, which make me tremble. Who could think calmly of the destruction of these marvels, products of an art, a man and a period all alike privileged? That period is gone for ever, nothing like it can ever reappear—taste and ideas diverge further from it daily, and create a wider barrier than time itself. But I must not run on thus. Let us go together to the Pincio. This afternoon, about four o'clock, coming from S. Peter's, I went up there. The weather was dark and cold, the walks deserted, the leaves falling heavily, and even at Rome it is winter! I stopped and gazed with feelings which I cannot describe, but which you will understand, upon the beauties I used to gaze upon ; but with what a difference ! Formerly time and hope were before me, and now they are both left behind. Ah ! there is the winter again ! Never mind, if we know how to accept our lot wisely, there is yet happiness in store for us ; so let us be wise !

"In a dark hour like that the green of the laurels and ilex is marvellous ; Mount Soracte seemed bathed in ultramarine, and behind Monte Mario the sky was simply golden. You can understand the harmony of such solemn yet rich strains. I enjoy such spectacles immensely,—I feel and love it all ; but I am doing nothing, and that is a cause of incessant regret to me. We have been here a month, and we have not seen one quarter of what we came to see, yet the time has been used as actively as we could manage. Is our whole time to pass like this ? I do not like to think so."

The account in Flandrin's Journal of their visit to the Catacombs of Saint Calixtus on Saint Cecilia's Day is interesting :—

"After Mass at the Trinità, all the family off to the Catacombs. Having passed by the Porta San Sebastiano, we entered the Via Appia, then an inclosure of land, through which we were guided by a row of box and flowers, up to the staircase, which was hung and lighted. The tombs in the walls begin at once as in S. Agnes, but here the quality of tufo gives a different appearance; the galleries are larger, loftier, and have a more architectural form. The effect of these fine lines, lit up with lamps here and there, is very striking. Not far from the entrance we came to a chamber or chapel in which is the niche where Saint Cecilia's body rested for long. This funeral bed was strewn with flowers, and lighted by a few flickering lamps;—it was very touching. On one side is an altar, where several Masses were said. At this moment a Cardinal, of noble countenance, was praying, his head bent upon his hands resting on the altar; we knelt down behind him, and so did several of our good little soldiers. The silence and darkness in such a place induced great emotion, and a solemn feeling of recollection. Little Paul gazed at it, almost scared, and fearing lest the excitement should be too great for him, his mother took him away. We visited galleries and chapels containing paintings with which we are familiar; tombs, rich sarcophagi still containing bodies intact. When we returned to the light, it seemed brighter, more golden, more cheerful than before. We went about a mile, beyond the tomb of Cecilia Metella, having visited the church of Saint Sebastian. The Via Appia, the town half hid behind its walls, the sacred wood, the

Campagna, with its long lines of aqueducts, and inclosed with mountains, all together made an entrancing picture beneath that light."

"*Nov. 30th.*—Vatican—the library—what treasures! I saw the Nozze Aldobrandini with great delight, but above all I was excited by a collection of pictures of Giotto, Gaddi, Memmi, and others of the same school, gathered together by Gregory XVI. The expression of strong and real feeling is carried in them to the sublime point."

On Sunday, Dec. 6th, Flandrin and his family were presented to the Holy Father. "We arrived at the Vatican at two o'clock, but were not admitted into the waiting-room till three; our friends the Pichons with us. The Holy Father received us kindly, and in a really fatherly manner. After we had kissed his foot and his ring, and while we were still kneeling, he pointed to my wife and children (as distinguished from our friends who had come first), and asked, 'These are your family? All these are yours?' and then, laying his hand on Paul's head, he added, 'May God bless you all. May your children give you every manner of comfort by being good children, and growing up good Catholics and good citizens.' Then he blessed our rosaries and medals, and on Auguste asking for a blessing on the Maison d'Auteuil, where he has been educated, the Pope answered, reaching out his hand, 'C' è.' Then I asked him to bless my painter's work, too, and he answered very kindly, 'I will invoke S. Luke, the patron of painters.' Then we knelt again, and went away to make room for other people."

"*Dec.* 11*th.*—Went to San Pietro in Vincoli. Hearing that the holy Apostle's chains were to be shown to some people, we joined them, and both saw and touched the saintly relics. A young Dominican, having put on surplice and stole, opened an iron or bronze chest in the thickness of the wall; then several little doors in succession; lifted a curtain, then a veil covering the reliquary, which is very costly; opened the reliquary with reverence, and displayed, ring by ring, the chains, which are carefully wrapped in fine linen. We began to hear the clink of metal, and at last, by degrees, the whole of the chains appeared. A young French priest came forward and knelt down; he kissed them in the official's hands, who touched his forehead with them, and put the collar which once fettered S. Peter's neck round his. Several priests and religious came up successively; men, women, and children paying a like homage and receiving a like reward. It was a very touching picture, which brought tears to my eyes, and has left an impression I fain would keep."

It is impossible to pass over the cloud which meanwhile was dimming what would have been a time of so much enjoyment, and which might have gone far to restore health to Flandrin's worn physique. It was the conscientious devotion which he always entertained for all that affected the growth and prosperity of high religious art in France, which made this cloud press so darkly upon him. There had been a series of administrative innovations in the Academy and the École des Beaux Arts, which were held by many, and by none more earnestly than Flandrin, to be most damaging to the cause they loved. "The danger is imminent," he writes to M. Baltard, "of nullifying the Academy by excrcising rcforms, which have no better means of renovation to suggest than systems (*procédés*) and material means. The professors are to be of painting, sculpture, etc. The Report tells you why; —systems of painting, of sculpture, of architecture, nothing but systems. And they add, with respect to the teaching of the old school, that it consists, strictly speaking, in nothing but a course of drawing well. I am ready to maintain that the school had at least the merit of recommending and of pointing out what really is art, and the whole of art. It is by drawing that life and beauty are expressed, the most exquisite delicacy, the truest philosophy. What remains after that? A garment, which I am far from despising, but which is as a necessary consequence of true drawing in high art.[1] And then they talk of originality, and formularise it, as if it was a thing that can be taught. They aim at organising freedom of teaching in a school, as though *le pour et le contre* given both at once could create anything but doubt! I believe that there, as elsewhere, it is a duty to teach nothing save incontestible truths, or at least such as are upheld by the highest examples, and endorsed by ages. You may be certain that the pupils of such a school will mould the truths of their own day to these noble traditions; and there you have a promising truth, because it is the product of real liberty.

"It is clear affirmation which teaches, not doubt. Do not be afraid of teaching respect and veneration for things which are really beautiful, by the position assigned to them, the care taken of them. Let it be clearly known that it is these that should be loved, admired, honoured. . . . No, indeed, everything is

[1] M. Delaborde remarks that this opinion of Flandrin's was no less unequivocally that of Leonardo da Vinci and Poussin. Leonardo says, in his Treatise on Painting, that "students aiming at rapid progress in the science which teaches us to imitate and represent nature's works, should devote themselves chiefly to drawing." And his biographer writes of Poussin, that "as he advanced, he devoted himself especially to beauty of form and correct drawing, which he recognised as the chief point in painting, and for which the greatest painters have almost forsaken everything else so soon as they understood wherein the true perfection of their art lies."

not equally beautiful, and you cannot put a *chef-d'œuvre* of Clodion and one of Phidias in the same category, as men affect now to do."

On receiving the Report announcing the proposed changes in the constitution of the French Academy, Flandrin wrote to M. Ingres:—"It was the very day after I had poured out to you all my delight in being here again, and my admiration for all which is the *raison d'être* of our dear Academy, that I received the bad news of these measures, which will upset it all, and will, I greatly fear, ruin our schools. Without entering upon a criticism of the Report, I want, my dear master, to tell you of the answer I have felt bound to give to the letter in which the Ministre des Beaux Arts announced the suppression of our functions at the École, and my appointment as *chef d'atelier* under the new organisation. There were more sides than one to the question, and I did not know what was going on in Paris, or what the Institut might do. But, all the same, taking counsel with what seems to be the honour of the Academy and my own, I answered His Excellency that I was gratified by this mark of confidence, but that I had combated these now prevailing views too long and too openly to be able honourably to support them now. . . . I hope and believe that you are on the same side, and will not disapprove what I have done."

By the same post Flandrin wrote to M. Gatteaux:—"For the last ten days I have been going over with delight the lessons which antiquity and the great masters afford here. Kindled with enthusiasm, my respect and gratitude was increasing for the admirable institution of Colbert and Louis XIV.; for this school, which, in addition to the study of these *chefs-d'œuvre* in their original position, combines the untold benefit of a community life, enables men to share the result of their studies in various branches of art. It was just when I was more convinced than ever of the value of these things, that the tidings of the ruin of all our grand institutions came crushing upon me. I say the ruin, for the Report which leads to the proposed changes is as inexact in views as in criticism, and I do not see what can come out of it all but the most utter disruption and destruction. May I be mistaken."

And again: "For my own part, I could not hesitate a moment. I perceived the chaos about to ensue, and I have refused to take any part in it. This dear Académie de Rome, to which I have returned so lovingly, has also received a mortal blow. The reduction of the studentship from five to four years, and still more the permission to students only to remain two years in Rome, is a poison which will bring down its strength, and lead sooner or later to its suppression. I would I may prove mistaken! But I must say it again, my sorrow is all the greater because my enthusiasm for Rome has taken still deeper root since my return to it. Yes, indeed, Rome is a wondrous place, the value of which to artists I appreciate more than ever!"

Flandrin began to write on the subject, but with his usual modesty he refrained from publishing his opinions when M. Ingres had given public utterance to the views of the conservative party. "It does not beseem me," he wrote, "to try and add anything to his words." The notes which he had intended to expand remain, containing much the same ideas as those expressed in the letter to M. Baltard, quoted above. He repeats still more energetically:—"It is not doubt which will teach men, it is affirmation of truth; and for this reason I will take no part in a teaching which is without principle or belief. Since I have the happiness of believing, I will not say, 'This may be beautiful,' I will only say, 'This IS beautiful,' without having other influences, superior or not, blowing hot and cold, now on the right hand, now on the left, upsetting all my work."

All these matters were no mere passing interest or subject for conversation to Flandrin—they engrossed his mind painfully; and if the objects of art by which he was surrounded, and to which he gave his attention by day, somewhat distracted him, his nights were sleepless and troubled by the urgency of his feelings. "The surprise and real grief I have been feeling these last few days," he writes, "have upset me greatly. Long hours of sleeplessness weaken me, and I cannot regain strength." On Christmas Day he wrote to his brother, while Madame Flandrin and her children were at Saint Peter's, having been obliged to stay away himself in consequence of his suffering condition; and an increasingly melancholy tone creeps over his Journal and letters from the date of the ill-omened Report.

"*Dec.* 12*th.*—Went with Auguste to San Gregorio. Domenichino's fine fresco is very much effaced, but there is still enough to authorise one in saying that it is his finest work. The grouping has all the grandeur of antiquity, and the drawing is in accordance with the majesty of the design. We also saw the fine antique white marble table at which Saint Gregory used to serve twelve poor men. Thence we went to San Paolo and Giovanni. What peace and stillness! and how entirely one can understand those who have wished to lie there for their last sleep!"

"14*th.*—Walk by the Ponte Molle to the Villa del Papa Giulio. A young artillery officer was very obliging in showing it to us. The architectural ideas are fine, and the paintings, though only Zucchero's, afford some agreeable results and useful lessons. We returned by the Pincio at the hour when I have so often watched the sun go down behind Saint Peter's."

"15*th.*—To the Theatre of Marcellus, and San Bartolommeo, where I was greatly delighted with a chapel covered with frescoes representing the life of San Carlo Borromeo. The simplicity of composition, the truth of action and expression, and the lovely bits of landscape, reminded me of Domenichino. It is so easy and skilful, and such charming colour. Whose work is it? I must find out."[1]

"16*th.*—Returned with Auguste, to prowl about San Bartolommeo, where the exquisite chapel delighted me more and more; then to Monte Aventino. I tried to draw there, but I was too weary, and pains came on everywhere. I could hardly get home."

On January 2, 1864, Flandrin writes to his brother Paul and his wife:—"Our first thought yesterday was for you—then, albeit at Rome, one had to think about cards and visits. I began with our Ambassador, going with the Academy and its Director (I like still to feel myself one of the household), then to General de Montebello, etc. To-day we dine with Madame de ——, but the dreadful, destructive part of the business is, that at every house to which one goes one makes five or six new acquaintances, involving visits to be received and

[1] The frescoes in question are by Antonio Caracci, son of Agostino Caracci.

returned, and all that! In vain we try to keep them off —it cannot be done. It would be less of a burden if I were well, but for the last fortnight I have had pain in my head, and a buzzing in my ears, which reduce me to something very like an idiot! My intellect is about as much obstructed as my hearing, and the people who want to make acquaintance with this 'celebrated artist' must be somewhat surprised at what they see of him, or can get out of him. *Ci vuole pazienza!* but on such occasions that is not my strong point."

"ROME, *Jan.* 9, 1864.

"To-day, in fine but cold weather, wrapped up as if we were going off to Siberia, we went in an open carriage by the Corso, the Forum and San Giovanni in Laterano, stopping to admire the view you remember in front of the church. For the last week the mountains have been white with snow—Monte Cavo covered from summit to base. But it was glorious under that bright sunshine. From the Albano road, a little short of the Tavolata, we turned up to the left, along a way which formerly was only to be distinguished by a few tumuli, which I remember well; but during the last five years, some slight excavations have easily brought the old pavement to light. Most interesting tombs have been found on either side; two especially delighted us, not only from their good preservation, but from the character of their rich decoration. I don't think finer specimens of this kind of monument can be found anywhere. We were deeply impressed, and little Paul, who had been lost in gazing with open mouth, suddenly exclaimed to himself as we reascended the steps which led to daylight: '*O pour le coup, ceci est beau!*' Indeed, his enthusiasm for antiquity goes so far that he looks upon the day as lost which is not devoted to the Campagna, or the buildings or excavations in Rome,—everything else is a mere accessory. Nothing can be more comic than to hear him declaiming archæology and history in the kitchen, classifying the buildings of the Republic, drawing his inductions from this or that style of construction. When he does not know anything about it, he invents —nothing stops him, *c'est à pouffer!* But he is not quite so keen and energetic when he has really got to earn something. It was quite a fête-day, for in the evening we went *al nobile teatro d' Apollo,* where we had Verdi's Trovatore, and the ballet of Cristofo Colombo, where I came once more upon the pantomime and costume which used to amuse us so much of old. Oh, the Court of King Ferdinand and Isabella, and the Turks, such as could by no possibility be found anywhere but here! I beg Rome's pardon, but you see, fortunately, she has other merits than these!"

"*Jan.* 14, 1864.—We are almost as much plagued here as at Paris! the numbers of people with whom we have been obliged to make acquaintance are past telling. One was obliged to go to the Academy, the Embassy, and General de Montebello, commanding our army, and out of these three roots a thousand branches have sprung. You are introduced to M. or Mme. So-and-So; they call upon you, you must return the visit, and the number of these new acquaintance is so great that I really do not know half the people again;—it is a real worry, and not one of our own seeking I can assure you; but how can we help it? You know how I care for our soldiers,—the sight of our flag, especially in a foreign land, is quite a religious, sacred attraction for me. There are so many here. . . . . I often admire their vigour and life; and it is an edifying sight too to see them filling the Church of Saint Louis, and listening to their chaplain (who, by the way, is worthy of his mission) with a respect and attention which move me greatly.

"You ask, dear Paul, whether I have found any of our traces in the Coliseum? No. A great deal has been done which somewhat interferes with the picturesque, but which anyhow tends to support and preserve the venerable ruin. The arcades you allude to have been closed by walls. This morning I went to the Academy by the Salita. The Pincio was nearly deserted, the sky, intersected with long streaky clouds, bore a melancholy expression, and mist hung over the town; and amidst the vague sounds which rose from it, the sound of a bell, which I seemed to remember, carried me back with a wonderful illusion to the days when we were never apart, and had all things in common. O dear old fellow, if you only knew how I want you at every turn! The thought of my happiness in seeing you again is my only consolation when the prospect of our departure from Rome, which begins to loom in the distance, comes before me. What is the fascination this land possesses, that it takes such a hold on all who are happy enough to love what is beautiful?"

That happy meeting was not to take place in this world. Although his family and friends do not appear to have been alarmed, it is evident that, in spite of his enjoyment of "dear Rome" and her many interests, Flandrin's health was growing worse, and that only his energy and unselfishness prevented it from becoming more perceptible. He writes to his brother Paul:—

"*Jan.* 28, 1864.—. . . . After spending some time at San Giorgio in Velabro, I came away with a chill which I cannot shake off: cold, neuralgia, fever; neuralgia in the face so painful that I did not know what would become of me. I was half blind, half deaf, a very miserable sort of being indeed. I have been rather better since yesterday, and mean to go out again; the weather is inviting, it has become so warm, which indeed has its own dangers. Why is my health no better? I often wonder at it,—*ma ci vuole pazienza*, that is the surest of all remedies.

"Since I wrote last we have hardly made any distant expeditions. We go over churches, palaces, and galleries again and again, and in spite of the long time I spent here formerly, I find much that is altogether new to me, and undoubtedly I shall still leave much unseen. My regret at leaving Rome is so great, that I have to comfort myself with a secret hope of returning. I do not resist the hope, for it strengthens me, and what hope shows to be possible for me, it proves possible for you too. So don't let us despair, but let us fill our time in the best way and with the best things we can."

In his Journal the same constant sufferings appear.

"Palazzo Spada—cold fearful. Palazzo Farnese—the King of Naples not yet gone out, and we are told to return, but I was in too much pain. . . . I am almost blind and deaf. I went to the Pincio alone. It is sad not to see this bright sunshine. Everything seems confused and uncertain. . . . What a wondrous expression of grandeur and melancholy there is in the Roman Campagna! It is very different in fine weather, but this is quite as eloquent. . . ."

The Carnival came on with heavy snow, and on Ash-Wednesday, Feb. 10th, it fell and lay on the ground even in Rome itself. "In the plains and on the mountains," Flandrin says, "it is like Siberia, and my rheumatism does not like that, or rather I don't like it, for I am still deaf and stupid. I can only hope that it will not last."

"*Feb.* 17, 1864.—My dear Paul,—. . . . We shall really have enjoyed our absence very much, in spite of my bad health, in spite of *le monde*, and in spite of the weather, which has been very bad for the last fortnight. I told you before that we had made acquaintance with the Princess Czartoryska, who is good, pious, simple, and a wondrous musician. The other day we went with her to Monte Mario to see Liszt, who lives there in retirement. He received us very kindly, and after we had rested a few minutes in the humble room he occupies in the convent, he took us to the Villa Mellini. It was the first time I have seen Rome from thence, and I am not sure but that it is the best view."

"*Feb.* 26*th*.—. . . . I have done nothing for so long, and the consequence is a mistrust of myself which becomes downright weakness. I want to test by some real work the true state of the case. The last few days I have been trying to make some studies, but it is very difficult to manage one's model in a sunny room, where one's family is perpetually on the move, and I shall accomplish but little. Meanwhile the anxiety about the Pope's portrait presses; everybody speaks to me of it as of a thing in hand already, and my present attitude of reserve, excuse, and apology is untenable. The weather is detestable; it has rained more or less continually for five weeks. We have hardly had four or five tolerable days out of more than thirty; and moreover this poor country is afflicted with numerous crimes. People talk of eleven attempts at assassination during the last fortnight, of which some, unhappily, have been only too successful; and as to robberies, they are endless, and committed with incredible effrontery in church and house in broad daylight. . . . Ah, our times were better than these! One thing which has interested me more pleasantly has been hearing Mgr. Dupanloup's sermons in the Gesù. They were admirable, and the immense congregation testified its respect and admiration by the most constant attention and ever increasing numbers. All this bad weather is a great hindrance to us, we lose so much time, in spite of our efforts to use it well, and it really is unfortunate, for we have still a thousand things to do. Time rushes away rapidly; we have almost come to Easter, and if I am to do any work this year I must soon set about it."

The only paintings which Flandrin executed during

this winter in Rome were an unfinished portrait of his little son Paul, and two angels' heads, as studies for the decorations he had been asked to undertake in the new Church of Saint Augustine in Paris, which his friend M. Baltard was at that time building. He also made a drawing for a portrait of Madame Flacheron. But, independently of all the circumstantial difficulties which surrounded him, Flandrin's health was a daily increasing hindrance.

"My incapacity for work distresses me grievously," he writes to M. Timbal, on February 29th, "but Rome is always Rome! Yesterday, after a visit to Overbeck, who seemed to me younger and more alive than he was thirty years ago, we went with a French religious of the order of Saint Francis to study the Forum and its environs. There were four or five inches of mud, but a ray of sunshine broke through the clouds, and everything resumed its wonted charm. The trees in the gardens of San Gregorio showed their white blossom for the first time."

On two successive days, March 1st and 2nd, Flandrin went to San Sisto, to study Père Besson's paintings, which pleased him greatly; he notices their good composition and fulness of expression, and remarks that the medallions in grisaille "contain things of deep pathos and of an eloquent severity."

There is something touching in reading of this,

almost Flandrin's last expedition in matters of art, being connected with one who, like himself, though after a different manner, had devoted his talents and his life to God.

The last among his letters is to Paul Flandrin. He talks in it of "the coming departure;" and truly that was at hand, but not such as he expected.

"ROME, *March* 5, 1864.

"I am better, but still I cannot get my head right. My ears are stuffed, and I am strangely wearied by a continual dull noise in them. But this time no one can say that I have overdone myself; I have done nothing, hindered as I have been by various difficulties, and now our departure is close at hand! Anyhow we have seen and re-seen Rome well, and I cannot tell you the lengths to which my fanaticism about her extend! Everything charms me, touches me, and fills me with an intense desire to stay here. Of late we have been smitten with a special admiration for the regions lying between the Capitol and the Tiber, and the Porta San Paolo, San Sebastiano, Latina, and San Giovanni, that is to say, for that part of Rome which comprehends the Aventine, Cœlian, and Palatine hills, and the valleys dividing them. These grand ruins, convents, and solitary venerable old churches, all raised to recall the greatest events or the most touching memories of early Christianity, have a heart-searching eloquence which I would fain never forget.

"Yesterday Auguste and I (my poor wife was ill) went with M. Visconti, the antiquary, and some other people, to see the excavations, which have been making for some years in the site of the ancient Ostia. We went in a little open carriage. It was a fine day, and the Piazza Montanara was full of picturesque peasants; on to Bocca della Verità and Ripa Grande, where we turned to enjoy the beautiful view of Rome, of which you made a very good sketch. Coasting Monte Testaccio, we passed the Porta San Paolo, beside which the Pyramid of Caius Sextius rises; a little further on we saluted the chapel commemorating the parting embrace of Saint Peter and Saint Paul, then the great Basilica of Saint Paul, and then at last came out upon the bare, lonely Campagna, which stretched out in familiar sameness to the sea. Stopping a few minutes at the Osteria Malafede to rest the horses, our six carriages resumed their way; the Tiber widens, the marshes extend, the salt pool begins, and far off rises the castle with its magnificent pine tree, which you must remember well. We came nearly to the sea-level, cross the *Salini.* On the left the fine fir wood of Castel Fusano stands out, and besides the four or five houses which compose Ostia there is a little church, which recalls memories of

Saint Augustine and Saint Monica. After breakfasting at the Osteria, we went to the excavations, which are most exceedingly curious. One goes in by the street of tombs—the pavement is complete. You still see the ruts hollowed by the chariot-wheels. It is lined with interesting buildings. Then at the gate to which it leads, you find a corps de garde and custom-house, after which you get into the town, divided into several streets. Thence you have about a mile to go above ground to the further extremity of the ancient Ostia, where the other range of excavations is going on, the intention being for the two lines to meet in the centre. It is on this side that the baths, temples, the shops which used to line the quays and port, are found, decorated with paintings, and very good and well preserved mosaics. This excursion was made much more interesting and useful by M. Visconti's explanations as we passed from point to point.

"Our return, from three to six o'clock, just at the most beautiful part of the day, was quite delightful. The grand and lofty points of view were enhanced by the flocks with their lambs and colts, and by the abundant flowers. Everything seemed to be crying out, Spring is coming! I must confess to you that I was quite overcome, and I can see a tear of sympathy fall from your eyes. Adieu, my Paul. Kiss

Aline and the little ones fondly for us; we love you so dearly.—Your devoted brother and friend."

We need scarcely ask to be forgiven for a repetition of the latter description, in words nearly identical, when we say that they are the last Flandrin ever wrote in his Journal:—"It was three o'clock, and so too late for Castel Fusano, and we took the road to Rome, turning towards the mountains, and leaving the sea behind us. *C'est la belle heure.* A soft sunshine made the whole world glad with its light. Flocks wandered in every direction, animated by the little ones—calves, foals, and lambs. The fruit-trees were laden with blossom, the hawthorn was bursting into flower, and all this grace, this youth, this resurrection, on the stern soil of the Campagna, had an inexpressible charm of contrast which was exquisitely pathetic and touching."

Pathetic indeed! yet not more so than the last loving looks of the Christian painter, seeing all things through the Vision of Beauty, which comes from Him Alone Who is the King of all Beauty, the Monarch of all true art, the Lord before Whom every treasure of intellect, brain, hand, or heart, must be laid and hallowed ere it can attain its true object—the benefit and enlightenment of man. But a few days later, and Hippolyte Flandrin was to enter the dark valley, whence he should indeed "leave the troubled sea of life behind, and turn to the mountains"—the Golden Hills "whence cometh my help." The soft sunshine of his beloved Italy would beam on him no more, but he was soon to enter there where the Sun of Righteousness is the light; his eyes, "dazzled now and weak," were soon about to—

> "See the King's full glory break,
> Nor from the blissful vision shrink:
> In fearless love and hope uncloyed,
> For ever on that ocean bright
> Empowered to gaze, and undestroyed,
> Deeper and deeper plunge in light."

He had struggled hard with failing health and strength; a vivid sense of duty had upheld him from giving way to the infirmities which were making his "clay cottage to totter ere it fail."

Immediately after this expedition to Ostia, Flandrin became more seriously ill. "We were waiting for fine weather to go to Naples and Pompeii," he wrote; "the fine weather has come, but our plans have given way before my illness, and now everything is uncertain."

Not for long was the uncertainty. A few days more, and the distressing symptoms, which at first seemed only an aggravation of what he had suffered for months past, developed into smallpox. It was not a very severe attack, and on the sixth day after the malady appeared

Flandrin was better, he took some food, and all seemed to be going on well.

"Yesterday" (so writes a student of the Academy, M. Bourgaux, to Ambroise Thomas) "I went to his house at five o'clock, and found him in his last agony, while, sad to say, his family had no idea that death was so close at hand. The servants had sent for an Italian priest, who, on arriving, said that extreme unction should be instantly administered. That was just when I happened to come, and I ran hastily to a neighbouring church to summon the last succours of the Church to the dying. Two hours later he was dead."

The last words he uttered betokened how the faith which had moulded and strengthened his life now sustained and brightened his deathbed. "I see the road, a saint is leading me!" he whispered in faint accents shortly before his death; "I see the road, it is made ready!"

The silver cord was loosed and the golden bowl broken, and the weary spirit had found rest for ever

In Patria.

A little later and the painter returned to Saint Germain des Prés, where his work was yet unfinished, yet all his earnest aspirations were fulfilled. His earthly remains rest there, where his own brush has raised his best monument.

A few earnest words spoken by M. Beulé at Hippolyte Flandrin's funeral may be quoted here.

"We have lost," the speaker said, "we have lost one after another, in rapid succession, Ary Scheffer, Delaroche, Decamps, Horace Vernet, Delacroix, and now Flandrin—the youngest, but not the least important; Flandrin, who was revered by all opposing parties; Flandrin, who upheld the standard of the ideal and of religious art with a hand as modest as it was firm; Flandrin, whose bright talent, always advancing, rising year by year to a more radiant height, seemed only as yet in its first bloom! What works he was about to complete, or to begin! What immortal pages were yet to be written on the walls of Saint Germain des Prés and of the Cathedral at Strasburg! What a fertile maturity lay before him! . . . It were not seemly, amid these funeral rites, to dwell upon Flandrin's life or his works. . . . Let us only say a long farewell to the earthly remains which Rome would fain have gathered in with those of Claude Lorraine and Poussin, but which now the sanctuary of Saint Germain des Prés possesses. Ever present to our memory must be that gentle, melancholy, recollected face, which seemed to belong to one of a bygone age; to a Christian neophyte painting the Catacombs, or a mediæval artist decorating his monastic chapel with inexhaustible fervour. Flandrin was moved by a sincere piety, which knew no display, but shone brightly within; it was the source of all his pure, lovely inspirations, wherein the utmost simplicity of feeling was backed by profound science; wherein the purity of antique form was united to that of Christian spirituality. He had another rare creed which alone can make a great artist; he believed in the dignity of his art, in those unchangeable principles without which there is no beauty, in rules to which the loftiest intellect must submit, and hence the exquisite simplicity and unity of his life."

And in the few feeling words broken by emotion which Ambroise Thomas, that dear friend of so many years, added to those already spoken, he quotes a letter he had received from a young student:—"Say that those who only knew him at the last are not the last to regret him; say that there was never a day when his heart did not win other hearts by the warm outpourings of his lovingkindness; say that many a young artist carries about for ever in his memory, the friendly words which were suggested by his inexhaustible sympathy for the young, and his immense love for his art."

**R. I. P.**

MUIR AND PATERSON, PRINTERS, EDINBURGH.

www.ingramcontent.com/pod-product-compliance
Lightning Source LLC
LaVergne TN
LVHW010256110826
845151LV00004B/1486
*9781425521950*